Post-Cold War, Democratization, and National Intelligence

A Comparative Perspective

Post-Cold War, Democratization, and National Intelligence

A Comparative Perspective

Edited by
Jin-hyun Kim
and
Chung-in Moon

Yonsei University Press
Seoul, Korea

Post-Cold War, Democratization, and National Intelligence: A Comparative Perspective

Edited by Jin-hyun Kim, Chung-in Moon

Published by Yonsei University Press
134 Shinchon-dong, Sodaemoon-ku, Seoul 120-749, Korea
TEL: (82-2) 392-6201, 361-3381~2, FAX: (82-2) 393-1421

ISBN 89-7141-407-3 93340

Preface

The subject of national intelligence has long been considered taboo by academicians, journalists, policy-makers, and ordinary citizens in South Korea. This is due not only to public fear of national security and intelligence apparatus but also due to legal and institutional barriers. The domain of national intelligence was not open to public discourse. Democratization and the advent of the post-Cold War security environment have, however, demolished old barriers and opened new spaces for public discussions on national intelligence. By taking advantage of new internal and external milieus, a small number of political scientists, policy-makers, politicians, and journalists have formed a study group, the Korean Society for the Study of National Intelligence (KSSNI), to explore national security and intelligence issues. The group is an academic forum devoted solely to the study of theory and practices of national intelligence in the Korean context. It is a non-partisan research organization which is run by contributions from its members and the private sector.

The Korean Society for the Study of National Intelligence organized its first international conference under the title of "Post-Cold War, Democratization, and National Intelligence: Comparative Perspectives," which was held in Seoul, Korea October 8-10, 1995. The conference was well attended by scholars, policy-makers, and journalists home and abroad. The event, the first of its kind in Korea, also drew broad public attention. Leading mass media organizations such as Joongang Daily, Seoul Broadcasting System, and Sisa Weekly covered the event. This edited volume is a collection of the papers which were presented at the conference.

It was a challenging task for a small study group to organize a major international conference. Had it not been for generous support extended by several leading private organizations, the conference could never have materialized. On behalf of our society and conference participants, we would like to express our cordial thanks to Daewoo Heavy Industry, Joongang Daily, Seoul Broadcasting System, Korean Airlines, Kisan Corporation, and Sisa Weekly for their financial and logistic support. We would also like to acknowledge moral support rendered by those in the policy community. Young-chull Chung and Duck-man Choi deserve our special appreciation.

Several student assistants from Yonsei University also played an important role in making the conference successful. We thank Jai-young Lee, Hun-gak Chang, Hyo-keun Ji, Dae-yup Yoon, Hyun-hee Bahn, and Jung-mun Choi for their unfailing hardwork and devotion. We are also greatly indebted to Professors Jung-suk Youn, In-Taek Hyun, Woosang Kim, and Jung-hoon Lee for their active participation and encouragement. Finally, we are grateful to Judy E. Chung for her excellent editorial work as well as her assistance during the conference.

Jin-hyun Kim
Chung-in Moon

Contents

Chapter 1

Introduction: Post-Cold War, Democratization, and National Intelligence

Jin-hyun Kim*

The international system has undergone major transformations since the late 1980s. While German unification, the restructuring of the Eastern European socialist countries, and the demise
of the Soviet Union fostered the dissolution of the Cold War system, the rise of multiple poles of power has brought about profound changes in the international political and economic land-
scape. New terrain in international politics has also accompanied
shifting terms of engagement among international actors.

The United States has emerged as the ultimate victor in the
war of attrition, forging a unipolar moment of power unprece-

* **Jin-hyun Kim** is President of the Seoul City University and President
of the Korean Society for the Study of National Intelligence. He was Minister
of Science and Technology of the Republic of Korea.

dented in recent world history. Yet, the triumph has burdened the United States with a traumatic period of domestic and external adjustment struggling with the purpose of its power. Russia, once the formidable rival superpower, abandoned its imperial ambition, and is desperately seeking an inward-looking strategy for national unity and rehabilitation. It is more due to fragmentation of social fabric, economic downturn, and the loss of national purpose have been demoralizing the entire society and its people.

While old powers are struggling with the paradox of history, new powers are gradually surfacing. With its economic wealth and dynamism, Japan is making a prudent projection of its international power and leadership. China is also showing a calculated move toward regional hegemonic leadership by getting out of its dismal past. In addition, the rise of a unified Europe and new middle powers such as the East Asian Newly Industrializing Countries underscores shifting patterns of power configuration in the international system. Despite its unique position in history, the United States is not willing to project its hegemonic leadership, making the new power transition more likely.[1]

The systemic transformation has also produced new norms and rules of international interactions. The realist paradigm, which has dominated intellectual discourses on international relations since the end of the Second World War, seems less compelling. The image of anarchy does not seem to dovetail with empirical reality. Furthermore, military self-help and the logic of

---

[1] On this issue, see Ronald V. Dellum, "Toward the Post-Transition World: New Strategies for a New Century," *SAIS Review* (Winter-Spring 1995), pp. 93-111; Robert Kagan, "A Retreat from Power?," *Commentary* (July 1995), pp. 19-25.

the balance of power and alliance politics are not the only ways to ensure national survival. In the age of globalization, strategic interactions among nation-states are not the sole determining factor of international politics. Globalization has entailed the proliferation of non-state actors, which are interconnected through transnational networks. Norms of cooperation, manifested in terms of several international regimes, are as powerful as instincts of conflicts. Military self-help and geostrategic concerns are rapidly shifting to economic interdependence and geoeconomic concerns. *Pax Universalitas,* rather than the Hobbesian image of all against all, is likely to be a more accurate portrait of the 21st century. This does not imply an absence of conflicts in the forthcoming century. They will persist. Yet, the patterns of conflict and the ways of managing them will be very different from those during the Cold War period.[2]

Changes are not confined to the international domain alone, however. In tandem with international changes, several countries have gone through extensive domestic transformation. As Samuel Huntington aptly epitomizes, the third wave of democratization has swept many parts of the world.[3] For all its transitional setback and hardship, Gorbachev's perestroika and glasnost opened a new horizon of democratic changes in Russia. South Korea, Taiwan, Eastern European countries, and several nations in Latin America have also made dramatic transitions to democracy. Democratic changes have accompanied new opportunities and constraints in coping with national security affairs. The domain of national security can no longer be considered

---

[2] For an overview of debates on realism, pluralism and globalism, see Paul R. Viotti and Mark V. Kauppi (eds.), *International Relations Theory: Realism, Pluralism, and Globalism* (New York: Macmillan, 1993).

[3] Samuel P. Huntington, *The Third Wave: Democratization in the Late 20th Century* (Norman: University of Oklahoma, 1991).

deus ex machina. Accountability, popular support, and national consensus have become new guides for managing national security policy.

The rise of a post-hegemonic world order and sweeping democratic transformations have brought about profound impacts on the concept of national security. The traditional hierarchy of national values, which places military security on the top of national security agendas, has become increasingly blurred. For some countries, such as South Korea, military security still remains vital. For many, however, the ultimate primacy of military security has become questionable. Non-military concerns such as economic, ecological, social, and technological issues are now as vital as military ones.[4] Some scholars regard economic security as the foundation of the next security system.[5] Likewise, the nature of national security has become contextualized and expanded.

National intelligence is an indispensable tool for enhancing national security. Thus, the scope and function of national intelligence is by and large dictated by the nature of national security policy. During the period of the Cold War, every nation was virtually obsessed with the collection and analysis of political and military intelligence. In the new era of fierce economic competition and waning military conflicts, however, many nations are shifting their attention from political and military concerns to economic and technological ones.[6] In some countries, national

---

[4] See Edward Azar and Chung-in Moon (eds.), *Third World National Security* (London: Edward Elgar Press, 1988).

[5] Berkeley Roundtable on Political Economy (eds.), *The Highest Stake: The Economic Foundation of the Next Security System* (New York: Oxford University Press, 1992).

[6] See Randall M. Fort, *Economic Espionage: Problems and Prospects* (Washington, D.C.: Consortium for the Study of Intelligence, 1993). Also see

intelligence has also become a primary vehicle for ensuring social order and stability by directly engaging in the prevention of terrorism, drugs, and international organized crime.

During the period of high military tension, the national intelligence system was insulated from social and political pressures. In the name of national security and secrecy, national intelligence organizations enjoyed enormous freedom in carrying out their missions, often resulting in the abuse and misuse of the public power extended to them. Democratic reforms no longer allow such a privileged position wrapped in secrecy. They are not institutional islands separated from the rest of society and politics. Though the extent of separation and secrecy varies by country, the conduct of national intelligence is increasingly subject to domestic legal and institutional constraints. Openness and accountability have become new norms for national intelligence systems in many nations.[7]

Papers collected in this volume address these timely and salient issues from comparative perspectives. In chapter two, William Colby presents a history of U.S. intelligence in light of four "revolutions"—from its traditional purpose to obtain advantage over an adversary to its new objective to establish the facts, from which parties can negotiate differences and come to solutions. This new approach, emphasizing knowledge and confidence, goes further in a positive direction than the original aim to seek momentary advantage that emphasized ignorance, fear, and suspicion. Colby carefully elucidates each revolution of American intelligence, beginning with the creation of the service in the first revolution, then its large growth in budget,

---

Warner's chapter in this volume.

[7] See Glenn Hasedt (ed.), *Controlling Intelligence* (London: Frank Cass, 1991).

importance, and inclusion of technology to obtain information in the second. The third revolution was a response to the challenge of how to protect the secrecy of intelligence while assuring that it functioned properly and democratically according to the American Constitution. The end of the Cold War necessitated a fourth revolution that goes beyond secret and technological means to agreement and acceptance between antagonists.

Colby is sure to point out both the necessity of any intelligence service to conform to the trends toward more democratic norms, and the fact that they are strengthened, not hindered, by public understanding and proper democratic controls. Having served the United States as Director of the CIA, Colby brings a well-informed stance to what intelligence should and should not do.

In chapter three, Vadim Kirpitchenko, who still serves as an advisor to the Russian foreign intelligence service, raises the importance of two aspects of national intelligence services in any democratic state. First, national intelligence service is an indispensable attribute of national survival, and second, its activities must be carried out in a civilized manner and under the control of legislative and executive authorities. Kirpitchenko traces the history and transformation of intelligence in the former Soviet Union from the Cold War, when activity was based on a "gallery" of enemies, to Russia in the present, when the goal is not to deal with foreign enemies, but to open up their own society, integrate into the world community, and redefine threat perceptions in line with the changed security environment.

Kirpitchenko stresses that unlike the KGB, the current Foreign Intelligence Service is a fully independent organization that serves only the legal constitutional structure of the state, both legislative and executive branches. Although the danger of global nuclear war has diminished, he argues that eventual military danger cannot be disregarded by any nation; thus obtaining information and maintaining state defense capabilities are still vital. As long as there are states with their own national interests, intelligence will exist as an integral part of the state apparatus. However, it is vital that they employ civilized methods in their intelligence gathering and that they abide to laws that regulate their activites.

While Colby and Kirpitchenko by and large address impacts of domestic political structure on national intelligence, W. Bruce Weinrod and Aviezer Yaari discuss implications of external changes for national intelligence reforms in the U.S. and Israel. In chapter four, W. Bruce Weinrod defends the need for the U.S. to maintain strong and effective intelligence capabilites if it is to remain a global power and international leader and maintain its alliance and security commitments in the post-Cold War world. If the Cold War and Soviet threat provided U.S. intelligence with a clear and set strategy, domestic factors and the international arena and the role the U.S. decides to play within it will decide post-Cold War U.S. intelligence policies. Weinrod covers how the U.S. intelligence service will develop and reform by discussing the changing international and domestic arena.

Weinrod covers issues ranging from the shift in the geostrategic situation and threat perceptions to domestic budget constraints; from emergence of low level conflicts to the new Republican congressional majority; from the emergence of transnational challenges to the CNN factor. However, he asserts that even the best intelligence can be ambiguous, thus, policymakers must be the ones to make key judgements and decisions. He concludes that U.S. intelligence will undergo changes as it must bear the burden of justifying and proving its worth in the post-Cold War era.

In chapter five, Aviezer Yaari presents a penetrating analysis of the Israeli national intelligence system. He explores the
questions raised about the proper role of contemporary national
intelligence in the post-Cold War era—what issues remain relevant, which have become more acute, and which have newly
emerged-as seen from the Middle East perspective. Using the
experiences of Israeli development of its national intelligence
service, Yaari suggests three main lessons learned regarding
intelligence: the need for pluralism in any intelligence system;
the need for long term as well as daily research of factors that
lead to war or peace; and the awareness of the dangers of preconceptions in intelligence assessment.

Yaari discusses the reasons why intelligence must be well-
informed about weapons and technology used on the modern
battlefield, using in part lessons learned from the Persian Gulf
War. He details current weapon capabilities to emphasize the
need for intelligence to protect nations against such highly
advanced arsenals. He concludes with a discussion of three
classical issues faced by intelligence: the need for human intelligence (HUMINT), the fundamental constraints on supplying
solid predictions of future developments, and the need to
improve the role of intelligence in the evaluation of national
policy.

Chapter six by Chung-in Moon, In-Taek Hyun, Woosang
Kim, and Jung-hoon Lee deals with the evolving nature of
South Korea's national intelligence system. They argue that
the national intelligence system in South Korea has been indispensable to national security because of acute military threats
from North Korea. Granted, authoritarian regimes abused and
misused the national intelligence and security apparatus for
the sake of regime security, critically undermining its legitimacy and accountability. Democratic opening in 1987 and the

new security environment, followed by the rise of the post-Cold War order, have brought about new challenges to South Korea's national intelligence system. On the one hand, it should regain public trust and support by severing the links between national security and regime security as well as by enhancing its accountability. On the other hand, it needs to not only broaden the scope of its activities by venturing into non-military areas, but also to diversify the methods of intelligence collection into technical ones. The survival and strengthening of South Korea's national intelligence system ultimately depends on two factors. One is reform from within, and the other is quality and commited political leadership to steer the intelligence community.

Weinrod, Yaari, and Moon et. al. concur with the idea that the traditional intelligence system cannot effectively cope with the newly emerging external and internal challenges and that it should undertake drastic institutional reforms regarding goal orientation, tasks and missions, and organizational structure. In chapter seven, Akio Kasai echoes a similar tone in describing the case of Japan's national intelligence system.

One of these newly emerging challenges is the issue of economic intelligence. In chapter eight, William Warner discusses post-Cold War economic espionage, an important issue considering President Clinton's directive earlier this year to the CIA to assign high priority to 'economic intelligence.' Warner addresses whether in fact policy can settle the debates focusing on policy issues relating to economic espionage, and whether it can truly meet the challenges of the "New World Order" or "New World Disorder." In his discussion, Warner examines state-sponsored economic espionage activities of Russia and France and the efforts undertaken by the U.S. government to counter such espionage, in light of foreign and domestic counterintelli-

gence operations, export controls, and enhanced private industrial security. Warner finds that economic espionage targeting
U.S. industrial technology is likely to increase from its current
high levels. He argues that the global economy, being as open
and market oriented as it is, facilitates such espoinage, and that
to solve the problem, more aggressive policies must be undertaken.

In chapter nine, Kasai offers a rare insight into the nature
of economic intelligence in Japan. According to Kasai, Japanese
intelligence activities have been concerned primarily with collecting economic information during and after the Cold War.
Although the end of the Cold War meant for many countries a
great shift in their economic intelligence activites, Kasai argues
that in Japan, intelligence activites remain almost unchanged.
With its defeat in World War II and forced renouncement of
any future military aggression, Japan learned to survive solely
on its economy. Japanese companies, to survive, enthusiastical-
ly imported foreign technology. Quite naturally there arose
cases of technological plagiarism, which Kasai succinctly covers.

Although there exists a Cabinet Intelligence Research
Office, its scale is too small in the global theater; Kasai expresses
hope for its further development and growth to keep up with
what is expected from Japan in the post-Cold War era.
Companies themselves need to take more preventive steps
against leakage of information; yet, intelligence must be careful
in how far it goes in involving itself in economic information
collection.

In chapter ten, Jang-Hee Yoo discusses the substantial
increase in the importance of trade secrets in the post-Cold War
era. Information and technological know-how are of ever growing importance, as more countries as well as private firms are

investing in them. As well as reviewing multilateral efforts for the protection of trade secrets during the Uruguay Round negotiation, Korea's position and relevance regarding the issue are covered in chapter ten.

Yoo suggests that to promote fair competition and active research and development, the importance of trade secrets must first be recognized. To prevent in advance the leakage of secrets, he suggests improved education and better employee monitoring. For Korea, he suggests that all firms prepare themselves for liberalization and the opening of the Korean market, and for the Korean government to actively promote a trade secret protection system.

As the concluding chapter by Chung-in Moon discusses in detail, we can draw several interesting comparative implications for the study of national intelligence from papers presented in this volume.

First, the concept of national security is gradually being redefined. The traditional realist conception of national security is being increasingly challenged. The diffusion of globalization, the salience of non-military issues, and the proliferation of nongovernmental actors all necessitate a significant realignment of national security agendas.

Second, as with the concept of national security, the scope and role of national intelligence needs to be redefined. Political and military intelligence is still valid and critical, but preoccupation with it could undermine the comprehensive picture of national intelligence. A National intelligence system should be prepared for dealing with diverse issues ranging from political-military to economic, technological, social, and even ecological ones.

Third, no matter how important the maintenance of secrecy is, the operation of a national intelligence system should not go beyond domestic legal and institutional boundaries. In the brave new world of democratic opening, a national intelligence system cannot survive without sustaining public support. Public support can be achieved only when and if national intelligence system abides by the law and ensures public accountability. In this regard, executive control and congressional oversight over national intelligence system serve as essential prerequisites.

Fourth, though not covered in the papers presented in this volume, participants in the conference have all emphasized the importance of intelligence cooperation among nation-states in the post-Cold War era. It is through intelligence apparatus that external threats are perceived and assessed and that national security policy is ultimately shaped. Lack of communication among intelligence communities and subsequent misperception and miscalculation could easily fuel conflictual relations among nation-states, and vice versa. Thus, enhancing communication and cooperation among and between intelligence communities of different nations could play an important role in cultivating peace and stability in the international system.

Finally, all of this brings up the necessity of reforming and realigning national intelligence systems. Shifting national security goals and national intelligence objectives, broadened targets of intelligence collections, diversified methods of intelligence collection, and democratic mandates for openness and public accountability all make reform of national intelligence systems unavoidable. As several contributors in the volume suggest, however, the nature and direction of intelligence reforms cannot be universal. They should be contextualized in light of the security environments peculiar to each nation.

Chapter 2

Democratic System and National Intelligence:
The American Experience in
Comparative Perspectives

William E. Colby*

Is intelligence work compatible with democracy? Many of its critics would contend that it is not. Their thinking stems from a basic syllogism:

> Democratic government is controlled by the people.
> The secrecy of intelligence work conceals it from the people.
> Thus the people cannot control it and a democracy can not permit it.

As with many syllogisms, this one is simple, clear and

---

* **William E. Colby** was Director of Central Intelligence Agency (CIA) from 1973 to 1976. He is currently Counsel to the law firm of Donovan Leisure Newton & Irvin as well as Editor of the Colby Report for International Business.

wrong. Democratic governments have conducted intelligence activities for centuries, and maintained their secrecy without derogating from their status as democracies. An early American comment on the subject makes clear their importance and their need for secrecy:

> The necessity of procuring good intelligence is apparent & need not be further urged All that Remains for me to add is that you keep the whole matter as secret as possible. [George Washington, 1777]

In fact, the American democracy maintains a number of secrets, for the simple reason that some government processes could not work effectively if they were conducted in the open. Thus the deliberations of the Federal Reserve Board are secret, the internal documents of the White House making recommendations to the President are privileged and military defense plans are prepared secretly. Systems have been developed over the years to ensure accountability and responsibility for such activities, but their secrecy remains protected.

When intelligence was revived as a major national function by the U.S. during and after World War II, the understanding was general that its necessary secrecy required that knowledge and decisions about it should be left to the President and the Executive Branch. The legislation it needed to exist as a part of the government and to receive and spend appropriations was drafted in the most general of terms, and the Congress hardly debated or considered what the Executive presented as necessary. Respected Senators proclaimed that they did not want to know the secrets of intelligence, so they would not have responsibility for them. And in the Cold War atmosphere, public support for this approach was general.

Another factor reinforced this attitude. Espionage is an illegal, even criminal, act in most nations. And yet it was clear that the U.S. would be conducting such actions around the world. The Congress and the Executive agreed that the new CIA would have "no police, subpoena, law-enforcement powers, or internal-security functions," making plain that its activities would take place abroad and barring it from actions against U.S. citizens in the U.S. But the underlying assumption was that its actions against the law in other nations would proceed. The only way such "lawless" or "illegal" activity could be justified was that the sovereign state had a right to break such foreign laws in the interest of its national security. For many years, therefore, the concept governed that law and intelligence existed in separate compartments, having little relation with one other.

But during these years American intelligence was changing. While it still sought and managed the traditional spies, it was growing into a much larger and more important institution in the American government. Its original character as a traditional small spy service reporting only to a King, a Prime Minister or a President was becoming a vestige of the past.

The first "revolution" in American intelligence began in 1942, when General William Donovan was asked by President Roosevelt to establish an intelligence service for the nation to meet the challenges of World War II. Donovan was a true hero from World War I, with the Medal of Honor and Distinguished Service Cross gained on the battlefields of France, so he was a fitting leader of America's efforts to develop spies and guerrilla leaders to fight Nazi Germany and imperialist Japan. But he was also a great student of foreign affairs, an avid reader and indefatigable traveller. When he formed the Office of Strategic Services, therefore, he arranged that its networks abroad be

supplemented by a great "center" of analysis in Washington.
These analysts were told to review all information, not just the
secret reports, available in libraries, geographic societies, corporations doing business abroad and known by hyphenated
American citizens about their homelands around the world.

Thus analysis became the "center" of this modern intelligence service. Donovan's initiative was followed in the years
since, and intelligence is no longer a simple spy service but a
major center of information and analysis of all sorts. As such,
its products became far more important to the U.S. government than individual reports from spies and were important
building blocks to major policy decisions taken in subsequent
years.

During the 1950's, a second major "revolution" in the intelligence discipline took place. Ironically, it stemmed from the
inability of old-fashioned spies to penetrate the harshly closed
fastness of Stalin's Soviet Union and its satellites. Communist
discipline and indoctrination brought swift exposure of
American attempts to insert such spies. And yet the need for
knowledge about the capabilities and plans of that great world
power was intense, with the Red Army threatening to overrun
Western Europe. A similar intense discipline had been imposed
on China with the victory of Mao Zedong there.

Faced with these frustrations, American intelligence turned
to technology to discover what it needed to know about these
areas which were "denied" to normal intelligence collection.
The most prominent of its products was the U-2 aircraft, which
flew over the U.S.S.R. and brought back photos of bases, new
weapons and troop dispositions. When it was shot down in
1960, the work was continued by launching into space the first
photographic satellites. Soon, this sort of technology was
matched by the growth of electronic monitoring in vast scale,

supplemented by the arrival of the computer age to manage and direct this enterprise. Other disciplines, from acoustics to seismology, soon joined the effort, producing a scope and precision of information for the analysts no simple spy was likely to be able to acquire or to transmit in a timely fashion.

These developments resulted in an even larger growth of intelligence in budgets and in importance, far beyond that expected from a simple spy service. It remained within the "central" discipline of intelligence, however, as only there could its results be consolidated with all other information by the analysts.

During the Cold War, another development increased the importance and controversial nature of intelligence. In response to the extensive subversive, political and paramilitary efforts of the Soviet bloc, CIA was called upon to mount a number of major covert political and paramilitary actions. Some of these were quite successful, such as Radio Free Europe, secret support for the Afghan fighters against Soviet occupation and the Congress of Cultural Freedom and related efforts to contest the Soviet effort to capture the intellectuals of Europe to their cause. But some failed, such as the Bay of Pigs invasion of Cuba, the 1958 attempt to support a coup against President Sukarno of Indonesia and the "contra" effort against the Communist government of Nicaragua. When they failed, they attracted high political attention and even when they succeeded they raised questions of exactly how the U.S. democracy was making the decisions which led to them. The great publicity they attracted also led to an exaggeration of their role. False attributions of CIA responsibility for many other incidents in which it had no or a minor role led to more major political attention. The question was not whether some lonely spy might be permitted to operate outside the normal workings of the American democracy but whether activities of this importance should be decided without the participation of the people's representatives.

The questions raised by these changes in the nature and importance of American intelligence led to a series of public attacks on it as being an "invisible government," a "rogue elephant out of control" and a threat to the constitutional rights of Americans at home. Investigations into these incidents were conducted with great hyperbole, major TV coverage and considerable sanctimony by some of the investigators. They did find some examples of steps over the lines of propriety over the years of the Cold War, but certainly not the great threat to democracy they were initially envisaged to be. The clearest evidence of this was the fact that these reviews led to no real changes in the missions and structure of American intelligence, finding it still to be an important service for the nation.

But the investigations did lead to one major change, a third "revolution" in the discipline of intelligence. This came from the realization that intelligence might have to violate some other nation's law in order to conduct espionage, but that this should give it no license to violate U.S. law. This novel thought (for the intelligence world) was combined with the decision that intelligence in its modern posture was too important a function to be left entirely to the Executive, so that the Constitutional separation of powers should be applied to it as it is to the other aspects of the U.S. democratic government. The challenge was to determine how this could be accomplished without destroying the secrecy that is an essential element of the intelligence process.

Developing the mechanisms to do this took a number of years and some exercises in trial and error. But the result is a workable compromise among contrasting power centers which ensures democratic control but also protects the important functions and secrecy of intelligence. It offers a number of lessons to other nations as they confront the same questions, even though differences among nations will produce many variants of the American model.

A first step was to produce a charter for intelligence, giving more specific directives than the vague legislative phrases which were considered sufficient in 1947. In the U.S., this has been accomplished by a series of Executive Orders of the President. The Congress at one time attempted to develop a detailed legislative charter, but it gave up when faced with the complexity and the opposing interests and views of critics and supporters of intelligence activities. The Executive Order charter outlines the organizations engaged in intelligence, their functions and various prohibitions on their activities (e.g., they will conform to U.S. laws; assassinations are barred, etc). It also establishes the organizational relationships among the different agencies conducting or related to intelligence. It designates in a public document what intelligence will do and what it will not do, so that its mission and its structure are no longer hidden under a King's cloak.

The second requirement, also covered in the Executive Order charter, is the structure and process of political control of intelligence by the President and the Executive Branch. This includes the supervision by the National Security Council of the substantive work of intelligence and the authorities and responsibilities of the Director of Central Intelligence with respect to the elements of the intelligence community other than the CIA, for example, the military intelligence services. These are designed to bring all these services into coordination to avoid duplication or conflict. The Order also establishes an Intelligence Oversight Board reporting to the President with responsibility for providing an independent review of any charges of illegal or improper actions by the intelligence agencies. A separate Executive Order authorizes a Presidential Foreign Intelligence Advisory Board of private citizens to advise the President with respect to the efficiency and management of the intelligence community. As a last point, the Office of Management and Budget of the Office of the President conducts a full review of the intelligence budget before the President forwards it to Congress. While much of the actual work of this supervisory apparatus goes on in secret, the public recitation of the system for Presidential control over intelligence is reassuring in its thoroughness and places clear responsibilities for proper and efficient service.

An interesting side effect of these measures for full Presidential control and responsibility for intelligence is their elimination of the doctrine of "plausible denial" by the President of responsibility for actions of the intelligence services. This ancient doctrine stemmed from the relations among monarchs, whose intelligence services certainly employed spies against their fellow monarchs. But if one were caught, his monarch was expected to react with dismay that any such action could have been taken without his knowledge against the interests of a fellow monarch. The spy was disowned, left to his fate and the fellow monarchs could maintain their "friendly" relations unaffected. While U.S. intelligence tried to follow this doctrine in its early years, it collapsed before the demands of democratic government responsibility in the U-2 and Bay of Pigs incidents, when both President Eisenhower and President Kennedy determined that they must assume full responsibility for those intelligence incidents or they would not be fulfilling their Constitutional responsibilities to manage the American government.

Congressional or parliamentary supervision (I prefer the word to "oversight," which has a negative meaning as well as a positive) is something quite new in intelligence. For centuries, in the "Mother of Parliaments" as well as the U.S., intelligence was left to the Executive by consensus. But in the aftermath of the 1970's investigations and explosions about intelligence in the U.S., a process was developed by which Congress could exert a full role in supervision of American intelligence.

It is clear that the normal legislative process of open hearings, floor debates and active lobbying by interested groups are not appropriate for the secrets of intelligence, or they will be secrets no longer. It is also clear that a secret cannot be shared with all 535 of the full membership of the Senate and the House of Representatives, despite the occasional efforts of these bodies to go into secret session. Thus a middle way had to be devised, asserting the Constitutional authority of the Congress but protecting the necessary secrecy of the nation's intelligence system. It was found in the formation of small committees of the members of the two bodies, who were to be entrusted with the secrets of the nation's intelligence-and expected to keep them-and act on behalf of the full membership of their parent bodies in approving or disapproving the actions of the Executive in this sphere.

Several aspects of these Committees deserve special notice. They are "select" committees, signifying that their members are specially "selected" by the majority and minority leadership of their house. This is a protection against the possibility that the normal workings of rotation among committee memberships might place on these sensitive committees a Member who would not have the confidence of the House or the Executive branch that he would respect the need for secrecy of the nation's intelligence system. This process has been thoroughly vindicated as several strong opponents of intelligence activities have served on the committees but totally respected its requirements for secrecy.

Another feature of the operations of these committees has been their own insistence that their members undertake strong obligations to protect the secrets they learn. There have been a few violations of this obligation, but the committees have reacted strongly against the members who did so, including public expulsion from the Committee of otherwise highly regarded Members. In general, the word in the corridors of Washington is that Congress does not leak as much about intelligence as the Exective Branch. This may be true, although hardly reassuring, but it makes the important point that Congressional supervision may have a cost to secrecy, but that it is a reasonable one for the benefits of Constitutional rule in America.

It fell to me to be the Director of CIA at a time of the first major attempt by Congress to assert its Constitutional prerogatives over intelligence. As the storm loomed I determined that intelligence would gain if the committees investigating it had a comprehensive view of the importance and value of our intelligence system, rather than focussing only on the incidents in which it had gone astray over the years. I thus determined to be as forthcoming to their investigations as I could, hoping to put the mistakes and misdeeds in proportion as minor blemishes on a fine contribution to the nation's policies and interests.

But I did have a problem: I had some secrets to protect, the sources who worked with us around the world. I therefore visited the new chairmen of the investigating committees. I said I did not wish to contest their Constitutional right to know all about American intelligence, as that would lead to a stalemate between us which would benefit no one. And I added that I believed it in our interest that they have a full understanding of the contribution American intelligence had made to our and the free world's safety, as I thought they would be positively impressed by it. But I said that I had an obligation to protect the identities of the many people, foreigners and Americans, who served us at the risk that their exposure would be followed by arrest and prosecution for espionage and other crimes, warranted or not. Thus I asked for an agreement that in response to my being forthcoming, the chairmen would accept that the investigation be conducted without the exposure of these names. I clinched the argument by pointing out that I did not know the names either. As Director, I could learn them, but the discipline of the profession was that I learn them only if I had a "need to know" them. I did not need to know their specific identities except in rare cases, and I should not go through the rest of my life with these names in my mind. The agreement was made, and despite worldwide publicity about the investigations and our earlier operational history, no names were revealed.

This question of the extent to which the committees must be informed is not an easy one, and it has led to some confrontations over the years. Admiral Stansfield Turner, Director during the Desert One operation to rescue American hostages in Iran, has discussed publicly one of his problems. As part of the plan, he sent two young officers to land at the Desert One site in a small aircraft to test the solidity of the landing zone for the heavier aircraft which would follow in the operation. He did not inform the committees of this operation before it took place. He said he could not do so without telling the two young officers that he was doing so. If they had been captured in the process, would the committees have accepted his logic? Actually, I think so, but it is a close case.

Director William Casey gave a briefing about the CIA's plans for operations to help the "contra" cause in Nicaragua, and in the text of his general description he mentioned that "mining" would be included. When it later developed that these mines endangered neutral shipping, one of the committee Chairmen vehemently protested that he had not been informed as the law required. But the Chairman of the other committee, and one of the protester's own fellow members, said that he had noted the word, had asked what it included and had received a full briefing.

It is easy to say that good faith will overcome the ambiguities in such briefings. But in the crucible of Washington political disputes, it is easy for a slight omission of a detail to be taken as bad faith. The regularity of the process, however, reduces these to a small number, and the process essentially works quite effectively.

The important point about legislative supervision of intelligence in the American system is that it helps intelligence more than it hinders it. Yes, it is a nuisance continually to think of informing the Congressional committees of the many events which crowd the schedule of intelligence operations, and to distinguish the ones of no importance from the ones which blow up into a crisis later on and produce demands for explanations as to why the committees were not informed. And arranging the testimony or other ways to inform the committees does take substantial time. Busy operators are focussed on their operations, and they are reluctant to turn their attention to explaining them to outsiders and defend them for their imperfections when they are concentrating on making them produce at least marginally against great odds. But this is the endemic problem of life in Washington, where the leaders of their profession, intelligence, diplomacy, military or the civil specializations, must both perform their functions and deal with Congress, with the second as important to their effectiveness as the first.

But plainly the pluses outweigh the negatives for intelligence in the process. The independent review by Congress causes the agencies themselves to be more rigorous in their planning, knowing that the resources and the potential political reaction to their activities must be subjected to the Congressional review. And in some cases, the process has resulted in the withdrawal of a proposal, as a result of the criticisms raised during the review. In two cases, Angola and Nicaragua, the Congress has gone further to prohibit operations, a disappointment to their advocates, but a clear example of cases in which the people's representatives insisted that their judgement prevail as to the wisdom of the operations. One can imagine the critical outcry if the agencies had proceeded with these operations and been discovered doing them. And I remember at least one case in which the revelation of an operation resulted in a denunciation of it by a Committee member, only to be stilled when he was shown the briefing he had received long before the operation began.

One of the vagaries of Washington culture is that Congress has required that it be "informed" of significant operations, but that it need not "approve" them (except as they are reflected in the budget). This attempt to limit Congressional responsibility when something goes wrong does not work, as the Committees clearly could block the action after the briefing; allowing it to proceed is in effect a grant of permission, or approval. On the other hand, the Congress rarely takes an initiative of suggesting or requiring that the agencies undertake specific sorts of intelligence activities, following the old tradition (occasionally under attack in foreign policy these days) that the Congressional responsibility is to decide upon Executive Branch initiatives.

One situation which resulted in a major public airing of the relationship between Congress and the Executive was the Iran-

Contra dispute. These are acutally separate incidents, but were linked into one set on open hearings with the usual American sound and fury. The Iran aspect involved the Reagan Administration's effort to secure the release of a number of American hostages held in Lebanon by terrorists responsive to Iranian support and influence. The Ayatollah Khomenei government of Iran was totally unsympathetic to the appeals for the hostages' release, but the Israeli Government suggested that the hostages might be released if the U.S. would sell anti-tank and anti-air missiles to Iran (despite U.S. law and embargo). Missiles were shipped through Israel by the National Security Council staff, not by CIA, using a privately-organized "Enterprise" to do so. When initiated, no Presidential "finding" that the operation was important to U.S. national security was completed, although a later one asserted this retroactively. That finding was never sent to Congress, however. When the "Enterprise" proved unable to ship the missiles, CIA was brought in to help. CIA officers insisted that another "finding" be issued to cover their activity, but again this was never forwarded to Congress.

The affair then expanded to Nicaragua. In the early days of the Reagan Administration, CIA secured a Presidential finding authorizing it to assist "contra" forces against Communist Nicaragua. This became politically contentious, however, and the Congress passed a "Boland Amendment" prohibiting actions to overthrow the government of Nicaragua. For a time, the assistance continued, under the theory that the contras were not trying to overthrow the Nicaraguan government but only blocking its expansion into neighboring nations. This rationale fell apart, and Congress then passed a second Boland Amendment barring any funds for contra operations by any "agencies engaged in intelligence activities." The Administration then turned to the NSC staff to organize various sources of funds for the contras, on the theory that the NSC was not an "agency engaged in intelligence activities." One of these sources was the "Enterprise" and it began to use the profits it obtained from the Iranian arms sales to support the contras.

When this murky activity came to light, it generated a massive public investigation by the Congress and several trials of the various officials involved, which led to their convictions (later pardoned by the President). The overall result, however, was to reaffirm the democratic system requiring that Congress play a full role in supervising intelligence activities. It also showed the fallacy of thinking that the system could be circumvented, as the injury to the agencies involved from the affair was considerable.

The end of the Cold War clearly has great implications for America's intelligence system. CIA and the other agencies obviously played a major role during this period, identifying the threats posed by the Communist bloc to the U.S. and its allies around the world. They also played a major role in the several decades of effort to limit the dangers posed by this massive confrontation, by providing confidence that arms control and reduction agreements between the adversaries could be precisely monitored. This permitted restraint by the U.S. and its allies without the fear that the Communist bloc could obtain advantage by secretly cheating on the agreements.

In fact, this process has constituted a fourth "revolution" in intelligence. Traditionally its purpose was to obtain advantage over an adversary-to know something about him he did not know you knew. "Knowledge is Power" and similar phrases expressed this objective. But the arms control process has produced a new objective: To establish a solid factual base upon which parties can negotiate their differences and come to solu-

tions, and be certain of later compliance. This can replace ignorance, fear and suspicion with knowledge and confidence, surely a far more positive purpose than seeking momentary advantage. And this has permitted erstwhile antagonists to go beyond
secret and technological means to learn about each other to new
arrangements such as agreed and accepted inspection and monitoring teams and opening their societies to the exchanges of the
new information age.

But clearly the end of the Cold War does constitute a great
change for intelligence. With the opening of normal communications among erstwhile adversaries and the adoption of "glasnost" by Russia, much of the information intelligence had to
seek with such difficulty is now freely available to the media,
academics and diplomats. And much of the strategic information is now available to the "think tanks," the academic centers
and the research series now proliferating in the private sector.
One American Senator has developed the view that CIA thus
should be disbanded and the normal centers of diplomacy and
defense absorb its functions.

Others object saying that the world still presents hazards
and threats. Some nations and movements still consider the U.S.
the "Great Satan" and its terrorists and extremists endanger our
citizens and those of our allies. Some recalcitrant nations still
harbor the intention of proliferating nuclear and other mass
destruction weapons into their hands, to threaten their neighbors or those they oppose. Ethnic, religious and tribal hatreds
are all too prevalent, exacting their terrible toll in blood and
misery despite the opprobrium of the international community.
And who can guarantee that the benign attitude of some of the
former adversaries is now permanent, and that frustration and
ambition cannot lead to renewed attempts at domination.

But the case for a reduced and different intelligence effort in the post-Cold War world is still substantial. And the U.S. has determined to face the problem of what this should be in the democratic tradition it has established for its intelligence effort over the past years. A Presidential Commission has been established to review the fundamentals of America's intelligence needs for the coming years. Its members are appointed from both parties, some named by the President and some named by the leaders of the Congress. It has full authority to examine all aspects of America's intelligence machinery and its challenges. Its report is due in March 1996 and its main points will certainly be made in public, with perhaps some classified elements discussing questions and capabilities still requiring protection-but those will certainly be shared with the intelligence committees of the Congress. From this study, the Administration and Congress will formulate the future directions of American intelligence, with differences of opinion, compromises and some new and some old directions.

But the Congress is not leaving this important subject only to the Executive. Independent of the Presidential Commission, both the Senate and the House of Representatives Intelligence Committees are fully launched on their own independent reviews of the requirements for American intelligence in the new world situation. Some of their conclusions will coincide with those of the Presidential Commission, some will differ, and the final debate will include them all. Plainly the process will be a clear exercise in democratic control of intelligence.

*   *   *

In these past several years I have had the pleasure of discussing with many current and former intelligence officials of a number of nations the question of how to resolve the problems of democratic controls over secret intelligence and security services. Some were long established democracies, some were new entrants to that kind of government from harsher backgrounds. Clearly each nation will have different approaches to the process, reflecting its own history and culture. For example, nations with parliamentary systems do not generally have the same separation of powers the U.S. does, so they have to make special arrangements to establish supervisory committees which contain a mix of the government and the opposition, and cause them to cooperate rather than engage in their usual debates. Some nations have a special problem in that they have what can only be termed a "disloyal opposition," so that including its members in the supervisory committee is too hazardous to the operations the services must conduct. And in some nations the services have long been more powerful than the legislature, so the hope of controlling them is quite small.

But plainly the direction is toward more democratic norms in the world, and intelligence services will have to adjust to these. My point is that they can become stronger with the kind of public understanding and support proper democratic controls can provide, a major "revolution" in the discipline itself.

Chapter 3

Perestroika, Glasnost and the KGB:
Surviving Democratic Currents

Vadim A. Kirpitchenko*

Studying the role of the intelligence in modern society is, to my mind, of extremely great importance, all the more because this theme has for many decades and even centuries been in "the zone of silence." Legends were created by the activities of the intelligence services; public opinion was generally misinformed of the true role of the intelligence services within the system of ensuring state security.

It seems to me that conferences like this one must explain to the public two aspects of national intelligence services in democracies. On the one hand, they have the right to exist

---

* **Vadim A. Kirpitchenko** is Chairman of the Advisory Board of the Russian Foreign Intelligence. He served as First Vice Chairman of the First Directorate of the KGB in the former Soviet Union.

because they constitute an indispensable attribute of any organized state. On the other hand, intelligence activity must be carried out in a civilized manner and under the control of legislative and executive authorities.

On the initiative of various public organizations and scientific centers, conferences and seminars have of late been held with the aim of investigating these complicated questions. The first one was an international conference in April 1992 in Bulgaria: "The Role of the Intelligence Services in a Democratic Society" The conference was convoked by the U.S. public organization "The Center for the Democracy" and the government of Bulgaria. A number of states sent their top-level intelligence officers, consultants, experts and observers to take part in the conference. For the first time in history there were proclaimed principles which the intelligence services should observe in their activities. In their shortest summary these principles read as follows:

- the states must have precisely-shaped legislation concerning the intelligence;
- reasonable parliamentary control over the activity of the intelligence is necessary;
- the intelligence service must carry out its work by civilized means without resorting to violence, coarseness and blackmail;
- intelligence services in democratic states must pass from confrontation to cooperation in the fields that pose a threat to the entire mankind (terrorism, organized crime, narcomania and so on).

The recommendations of the Sofia conference fully correspond to the new principles which constitute the guidelines for the practical activities of the Foreign Intelligence Service (FIS) of Russia.

However before coming over to the changes that have taken place in the Foreign Intelligence Service of Russia in the last four years, I would like to recall some Soviet intelligence history to show you the role the intelligence has played in our state system and especially in connection with the fact that we mark the 50th anniversary of the end of the World War II this year.

Historical Origins of Russian Intelligence

During the time of the Soviet Union, the foreign intelligence was one of the instruments of ideological struggle on the international arena. Its adversaries during the first post-revolutionary years were foreign anti-Soviet formations whose core was, as we called it, "The White Emigration." Later anti-Stalin oppositionists of social democratic and Trotskyist-type were added.

The establishment of the fascist regime in Germany and the growing aggressive aspirations of Japan in the Far East created a new and real menace to the very existence of our state. Hence it is quite natural that in the 1930s the Soviet Foreign Intelligence faced a powerful enemy, fascist Germany, as well as those who supported or could support it in future.

The years preceding and during World War II proved the necessity for a state to have an effective and well organized intelligence service. In those years, the Soviet Intelligence was not a separate service. It was not large and was a component part of the USSR People's Commissariat for Internal Affairs. Nevertheless, the Intelligence informed Stalin and other leaders of Germany's preparations for war against the Soviet Union, and obtained information on military plans of Japan. Such information began incoming ten years prior to the outbreak of World War II. Unfortunately, the leadership did not attach due importance to this information; thus, the first year of the war with Germany was extremely difficult.

For a better understanding of the functions and tasks of Soviet intelligence during the war, I shall enumerate some of the most important directions of its activity:

1. The foreign policy of the more influential states of the world during the war, especially of the enemy countries, as well as of the anti-Hitlerist coalition ally countries.

2. Obtainment of intelligence information on specific plans of the German military command from different sources, both in Germany and in other countries.

3. Organization and carrying out of intelligence and covert actions in the territory of the Soviet Union occupied by the German forces.

4. Japan's plans concerning its possible entry into the war against the Soviet Union. Evolution of the Japanese political and military leadership views on this matter during World War II.

5. Information on the position of our allies-the U.S. and Great Britain-on the opening of the second front.

6. Scientific and technological information, primarily on new types of arms, military equipment and, most of all, on the research and development of the atomic weapon.

7. Preparation for the meetings of the Allied Powers in Teheran, Yalta, and Potsdam. Obtainment of intelligence information on the positions of the parties concerned and ensuring security of the Heads of States.

   As it is widely known today, Soviet Intelligence was the first to obtain the information on Hitler's plans to slaughter Roosevelt, Churchill, and Stalin during the Teheran Conference.

8. Intelligence information on German plans to conclude a

separate peace treaty with the U.S. and Great Britain.

9. Plans of the Allies and other states on postwar rearrange-
   ments in the world.

When speaking of Intelligence activities before and during the war, I cannot avoid mentioning that it was in Seoul that our residency at the end of the thirties obtained the text of the famous "Tanaki Memorandum," revealing the expansionist plans of the Japan military.

The anti-Hitlerist coalition victory in World War II, unfortunately, led to the end of the coalition itself. At the moment we will not dwell on the analysis of the initial causes of the "Cold War." Undoubtedly, it was due both to the fear of the West of the spread of communism to Western Europe, and to the fear of the USSR, devastated by the war, of a new nuclear threat. Naturally, for the intelligence services on each side of the "iron curtain," it meant the emergence of new powerful enemies.

Now the situation has radically changed. Under the conditions of current realities we have given up the former approach, when the intelligence activity was based, so to say, on a "gallery" of enemies. We used then the following intelligence operative terminology: "main enemies," "likely enemies" and simply "enemies." Nowadays our starting points are our national and state interests.

We are seeking to establish an open society in our country, to integrate into the world community and to avoid regarding any country or groups of countries as enemies. However, should someone infringe upon sovereignty or encroach upon the principles of world order, as provided for in the international law and to which we are firmly adhering, then we are likely to obtain adversaries.

As for regular intelligence activity, it is necessary to maintain the position of professionalism and not be carried away by propaganda. When reserving for himself the right to conduct intelligence activity and produce secret information, one should not, naturally, be surprised that others will do the same.

Russian Intelligence in Transition

Till 1991 our Foreign Intelligence was part of the KGB creating preconditions for its involvement in alien activities. In autumn 1991 the Committee for State Security (KGB) was disbanded and the Foreign Intelligence became an independent organization, oriented to work exclusively in the foreign sphere.

The counterintelligence departments of the former KGB have undergone a number of reforms and today they form the Federal Security Service of Russia. Their principle assignment is to impede foreign espionage and fight terrorism and organized crime. Also set up was an independent service, the Federal Agency of Government Communications and Information. The Frontier Forces, having to safeguard both the borders of Russia and the borders of the Commonwealth of Independent States, received independent status. On the basis of the KGB Directorate of Government Bodyguards there were established two services: the Security Service of the President and the Service of Government Bodyguards.

There arises a legitimate question, how is the national security of Russia being ensured under these conditions? Of course, when all these organizations lived under the same roof, the problems of interaction and coordination of all secret services were solved more effectively, though one cannot say that we had an ideal scheme. There are a great deal of issues today in relation with coordination and interaction. The reason for this lies both in the country's complicated political and economic situation and in the fact that these special services are still striving to find optimal ways to function.

Currently our special services activity is being coordinated by way of regular working meetings of their heads. There are a number of agreements and protocols signed between them; high ranking intelligence officers maintain contacts with representatives of other agencies.

The coordination function is carried out by the Security Council, which includes the "forces' ministers" (who represent the Armed Forces, law enforcement agencies and security), leaders of both chambers of the State Duma and other senior statesmen. The Security Council is headed by the President of Russia, and the special services are in direct subordination to him.

Having become an independent body, the Intelligence Service is undergoing deep transformations towards its democratization:

- a civilian, well-known scientist-politologist Evgueny M. Primakow, was appointed Director of the Foreign Intelligence Service;
- about 30% of intelligence officers have been discharged, more than 30 of our residencies abroad have been closed;
- we have rejected the so-called "globalism" in our activity. In the past our intelligence activity covered practically all countries; now they cover only those of intelligence interest;
- in Intelligence, departization has been carried out.

This requires some explanation. In the past almost all intelligence officers were members of the Communist Party. At present, for security personnel, party membership and activity in any political organization is forbidden. This has saved

Intelligence from self-destruction. Had the intelligence officers gotten involved in acute inter-party contest, now characteristic of our society, normal intelligence activity would be out of the question. However this does not mean that intelligence officers are prohibited to have political preferences. During referendums or elections of the members of the Parliament and other legislative bodies, each intelligence officer is guided by his own political views.

The transformation of the Foreign Intelligence Service into an independent organization has brought about both advantages as well as drawbacks. It is clear that while part of the KGB, Intelligence could easier coordinate actions with other services of the KGB. Unfortunately, new personal contacts between the intelligence and counterintelligence officers have been reduced. However, the advantages have turned out to be more substantial: all operational decisions are being adopted more rapidly, and most importantly, the Intelligence now reports information directly to the President and Prime Minister as well as different state organizations without intermediary authorities. Intelli-gence information no longer is corrected due to someone's conjunctural considerations.

Institutional Reforms and Russian Foreign Intelligence Service

Till 1992 there was no law on Intelligence in our state. Intelligence activity was subject to the instructions of the CPSU Central Committee and to the orders of KGB Senior Officers. In fact, an intelligence officer could receive the most unexpectable order and had to obey it. At the new stage of development of our state, particularly after the dismemberment of the KGB, there appeared a sharp necessity to create a new law on Intelligence placing it under the control of the legislative and executive bodies. At the end of 1991, special committees of the Russian Parliament together with foreign and military intelligence officers, began to elaborate the law. Those engaged in this work went on to study the legislation on intelligence in foreign countries. Here we came upon something rather unexpected. It was discovered that only in the U.S. did there exist detailed laws on intelligence. In some European countries there are separate legislative acts regulating some aspects of intelligence activity. But in the overwhelming majority of states there are no laws on intelligence at all, which might certainly lead to abuses and violations.

On July 8, 1992 the Parliament of the Russian Federation passed the Law On the Foreign Intelligence. Now it is clear to the intelligence officers what they can, should or must not do. At present, the intelligence activity is conducted in strict accordance with this law.

The main provisions of this law are the following:

- the Russian Intelligence acquires sources of information only on the basis of their voluntary consent; the intelligence activity should not pursue anti-human goals and should not risk lives or health of persons and damage to the environment. The intelligence activity, according to the law, is under control of the supreme legislative and executive bodies of the Russian Federation;

- the Intelligence must not take actions which could be considered as interference into the internal affairs of other states. Now we do not provide money and weapons to anybody, do not support any political party or unit on foreign territories. The intelligence function is limited to collection of information concerning only the security of our state;

- the Intelligence is prohibited from resorting to any medical drugs and forms of pressure on persons (blackmail, compromising materials, threats);
- after separation from the KGB, the Intelligence ceased to be part of the law-enforcement system and consequently cannot detect offenders, develop and arrest them, carry out investigations and refer cases to the court.

Redefining Intelligence Missions

As a result of positive changes in the world, the threat of a global nuclear-missile war and large-scale military conflict has been minimized. However, an eventual military danger has not yet been fully eliminated. Besides, there remains a possibility of development of new types of weapons no less frightful than the nuclear weapons. One should also bear in mind the possibility of obtaining mass-destruction weapons by those regimes which pursue expansionist policies or have territorial claims to other states. Local conflicts in the CIS in which Russia may be involved also cause concern.

Under these circumstances, the task of obtaining information contributing to the maintenance of the defense capability of Russia, its economic security and of such data on the achievements in modern sophisticated technology that may appear to be vital for our state, remains actual.

The shaping of domestic and foreign policy and independent adoption of decisions as to what does and what does not suit the national interests of the state is out of the sphere of the Foreign Intelligence Service. The Intelligence serves only the legal constitutional structures of the state, both legislative and executive branches of power.

Within such a comprehension of the international situation, and in accordance with the Law on the Foreign Intelligence Service and the directives of the Russian Federation President concerning the national security, the main lines of the Foreign Intelligence Service activities are the following:

- obtaining political information on the problems that are of the utmost importance for Russia's security;
- assisting the implementation of the foreign policy of the State of Russia by means of intelligence;
- science and technology line, including the national defence interests;
- safeguarding the Russian economic security;
- the ecological security;
- the questions of the intelligence activities' security;
- cooperation with the special services of other states.

As cooperation with foreign special services has obtained special importance in recent years, this line of the Foreign Intelligence Service activities deserves a more detailed discussion.

The Foreign Intelligence Service of Russia maintains professional contacts and partnership ties with dozens of special services of different states of the world, including the majority of NATO countries. These contacts are bilateral and of confidential nature and are based on the mutual interests of the cooperating sides. Such cooperation should not be directed against any third country. The typical points of cooperation are: exchange of information on the problems of non-proliferation of the mass destruction weapons, incumbent critical situations and existing crises (Yugoslavia, the Middle East, the Russian borders, etc.), the problems of mutual security of the states, exchange of information on terrorism, national extremism, narcomafia activities, organized crime and on other topics related to the criminal sphere. With a number of special services we have a regular exchange of experts, and mutual visits of the Intelligence chiefs are carried out on a planned basis.

The Foreign Intelligence Service is opened for new contacts, naturally, with those states that do not pursue policies of aggression and extremism.

We are of the opinion that as long as there exist states with their own national interests, there will exist intelligence services as an integral part of the state apparatus. But intelligence activity in this post-confrontation period should use only civilized methods, i.e. no "arm-twisting," threats, blackmail and rude pressure.

The improvement of the international situation and the transition from the policy of confrontation to the policy of cooperation have forced the special services of a number of states to reassess their doctrines and principles of work. Intelligence and counter-intelligence services have come to realize the necessity of adopting laws to regulate their activities. If these trends further develop, the intelligence services, whose activities in the past often caused complications in the interstate relations, may become effective instruments of the international stability.

After the breakdown of the Soviet Union and the formation of the Commonwealth of Independent States(CIS) there appeared the problem of how to build relations between the special services of the newly emerging states. It should be noted from the very beginning that the Baltic states of Latvia, Lithuania and Estonia have not joined the CIS. We consider them as independent foreign states that have no specific links with Russia as far as special services are concerned. As for those former republics of the Soviet Union that have joined the CIS, the intelligence and counter-intelligence bodies of Russia maintain close professional relations with them.

The CIS member-states have concluded a collective agreement on the cooperation in the sphere of intelligence activities. Besides this, the Foreign Intelligence Service of Russia has bilateral agreements with the majority of the CIS member-states. The Intelligence Services of these states have assumed the obligation not to wage human intelligence against each other. There are corresponding laws to this effect.

The cooperation of the intelligence services within the CIS framework envisages exchange of current political and operative information, mutual help and assistance by means of the operative equipment and machinery, permanent consultations on different levels on the questions of intelligence activities, and assistance in personnel training.

The further promotion of the cooperation between the intelligence services will depend on the development of the political and economical situation in the CIS.

As it is known, there exist opposing development tendencies within the CIS: some forces are pushing the young states toward a break off with the CIS member-states; at the same time the tendency for more close integration in the political and economical spheres within the limits of the CIS. It is clear that much will depend on the situation in Russia itself. If there is political stability and a revived economy in Russia, then the integration processes undoubtedly will proceed much more rapidly.

Assessing Recent Situations in Asia-Pacific

And now let me express some considerations concerning our assessment of the situation in the Asian-Pacific region. This region undoubtedly has become the world's most important political and economic centre in the past several decades. Russia seeks to have stable and balanced relations with all the states of the Asian-Pacific region. That would contribute to the successful progress of the reforms in Russian Federation and development of the unique Eurasian potential of Russia.

We seek to maintain close business relations with all our traditional partners in this region and to establish diversified links with the states which previously had not been in the sphere of our active policy.

One of the most important and perspective spheres of our activities in the Asian-Pacific area is the cooperation with the special services of the countries of this region in order to strengthen security here. We consider our special services capable of further developing the mechanism of multilateral negotiations on the problems of non-proliferation of nuclear weapons, in the first instance in Northeast Asia and on Hindustan subcontinent. It is necessary to establish a mechanism for prevention and settlement of crises with the participation of states concerned, and to carry out some other measures to guarantee stability and predictability of the situation on a regional and subregional level.

With this in view, the Russian Foreign Intelligence Service is building up partnership relations with the intelligence services of the Asia-Pacific region states in order to create favorable conditions for the solution of the following tasks:

- creation of prerequisites for involvement of the Asia-Pacific region states in the process of real nuclear disarmament and strengthening control over non-proliferation of mass-destruction weapons and means of its delivery. As applied to the Korean Peninsula, this means the observance of nuclear weapons non-proliferation regime and the implementation of measures to normalize relations between the two Korean states;

- settlement of territorial claims by peaceful means and on a mutually acceptable basis;
- active development of mutually beneficial economic cooperation on the basis of bilateral and multilateral economic projects and with the participation of regional organizations on the basis of equality without predomination of a state or group of states in the region;
- ecological situation in the region, forecasting of the threat of ecological danger;
- curbing the international terrorism, drug-business, organized crime, smuggling, sea piracy, unlawful migration of the population.

Concluding Remarks

The development of democratic processes in Russia brought about more frankness and glasnost to the activities of all state institutions, including its Foreign Intelligence Service. The Parliamentary Law "On the Foreign Intelligence Service" envisages introduction of the concept of glasnost in our Service.

The Intelligence is obliged, within reasonable limits, to inform Russian and foreign public opinion about its activity. In accordance with the law, a special body has been set up in the FIS framework, namely, the Public and Mass Relations Bureau. Everyday Russian and foreign correspondents turn to this Bureau in order to obtain current information. Scientists, historians and writers also turn to the Bureau for help.

In the past several years, owing to the fact that censorship on publications in Russia has been abolished, many materials on intelligence, distorting the real facts, have appeared in mass media. Thanks to the fruitful work of this Public Relations Centre, all sorts of falsifications and inventions in mass media concerning the activity of Russian Intelligence have been reduced.

The senior intelligence officials regularly make different reports, addressing the public and journalists. They also make television and radio appearances. For the last two years, the FIS Director, Academician Evgueny Primakov, has presented at press-conferences reports devoted to such problems as the non-proliferation of mass-destruction weapons, prospects of the transformation of NATO, and the situation in the Common-wealth of Independent States.

Some veterans of Intelligence have published their political studies and memoirs. At present we are preparing for the open publication the History of Russian Intelligence.

The Foreign Intelligence Service has a positive attitude towards invitations from scientific and public organizations of different countries. The FIS representatives make reports on the problems of the intelligence activity at international confer-ences, seminars and in university lecture-halls.

In conclusion, the Russian Foreign Intelligence Service has undergone a profound transformation in the process of *glasnost* and *perestroika*. Indeed, democratic change has remarkably enhanced accountability, openness, and depoliticization of the Russian Foreign Intelligence Service through a series of legal and institutional reforms. The trend seems irreversible, which will prove to be positive for peace and prosperity in Russia as well as in the world as a whole.

Chapter 4

Changing U.S. International Interests and Priorities:
Implications for Intelligence Reforms

W. Bruce Weinrod*

For several decades after the end of World War II, the U.S. had a defining national strategy based upon a clear and present danger from a global, expansionist-oriented and ideologically-driven Soviet Empire. This strategy also made it relatively easy to make decisions among competing international and domestic priorities, including the shaping and implementation of intelligence policy.

With the end of the Cold War, the U.S. public and policy-

---

* **W. Bruce Weinrod** is a Washington, D.C.-based attorney and an Adjunct Fellow at the Center for Strategic and International Studies. He served as Deputy Assistant Secretary of Defense for European and NATO affairs.

makers alike concluded that many elements of the U.S. Cold War posture needed to be reviewed and reassessed. Quite naturally, U.S. intelligence capabilities, priorities and programs are included in this overall post-Cold War reassessment process.

Many specifics of U.S. intelligence policy in the post-Cold War era will become clearer by the middle of 1996. At that time, the Commission on the Roles and Capabilities of the U.S. Intelligence Community, recently established by the U.S. Congress, will present its report and recommendations. The Commission, composed of 17 Presidential and congressional appointees and chaired by former Secretary of Defense Harold Brown, is reviewing all dimensions of U.S. intelligence. In addition, the House Intelligence Committee has also launched a review of how U.S. intelligence should be shaped for the 21st century.

However, it is possible even now to consider the challenges for U.S. intelligence policy. The likely direction of future reforms can be considered usefully within the overall context of the domestic and international factors which are affecting the development and implementation of U.S. foreign (including defense and international economic) policy in the post-Cold War world.

This paper will review first key domestic and international factors which are relevant to U.S. foreign policy in this new era, and it then will assess the implications of these factors for the future direction of U.S. national intelligence policy.

Post-Cold War International Environment

Post-Cold War U.S. intelligence policy and priorities will be influenced significantly by the international role which the U.S.

assumes and by the international obligations and commitments it undertakes. The following are important changes or developments in the new international environment and in U.S. foreign policy perceptions which are likely to affect U.S. intelligence policy.

Lack of Consensus Over U.S. National Interests and Role in the Post-Cold War World

An inevitable by-product of the end of the Cold War has been a reassessment of U.S. national interests and the proper American role in the post-Cold War international environment. In the early post-World War II period, of course, there was a clear and present danger of Soviet expansionism which necessitated the shaping of a coherent overall strategy—the "containment" policy—and made the emergence of a broad American consensus in support of this strategy almost inevitable.

At present, however, there is no direct threat to U.S. security, and the international situation as a whole is fluid and amorphous. This in turn makes problematic both the development of an overall U.S. strategy and a consensus in support of any such approach.

Shift in Geostrategic Situation and Threat Perceptions

For over four decades, U.S. intelligence priorities were shaped within the framework of one overriding priority—to deter, or if necessary, defend against, Soviet aggression and to counter Soviet efforts to extend its global influence.

The result was an intelligence community focused on political and military analysis of the intentions, capabilities and activities of the Soviet Union. At present, potential threats to

U.S. interests are more diffuse, and there is no immediate direct threat to the U.S. homeland although there still remain threats to U.S. vital interests, especially, the North Korean conventional threat against Seoul, and the North's nuclear capability. Aside from the situation on the Korean Peninsula, the U.S. should in general have more warning time to develop a response to any potential direct threat to its vital interests.

Residual Longer-Term Concerns: Russia and China

Even assuming the persistence of a more fluid international environment, there is likely to be general agreement in the U.S. that there remain two nations that could potentially pose a significant direct security threat to the U.S. in the next decade or two—especially because they both will possess the means to deliver substantial numbers of nuclear weapons onto U.S. territory. These two nations are Russia and China.

While neither nation currently poses a direct security threat to the U.S., it is inevitable that Washington will be very much concerned about developments within each nation and in their attitudes and policies towards the U.S.

Maintenance of Alliance Commitments and Structures

Although some Americans are suggesting that traditional U.S. alliances and other commitments are "relics of the Cold War," most Americans (and the U.S. government) still conclude that America's formal and informal alliance relationships around the world remain important.

Thus, even though the Cold War has ended, the U.S. views its NATO relationship as a linchpin of its relationship with Europe. Although the international environment has changed considerably, the U.S. regards its alliance commitments, such as to defend South Korea and Japan, as still valid.

Emergence of Low-Level Conflicts

While the possibility of another Persian Gulf-type or major conflict cannot be ruled out, more likely is that over the next few years, the U.S. will be faced more with what are sometimes referred to as "low-level conflicts." Such conflicts, while violent, are localized and relatively small and require appropriate intelligence community support and involvement. A current example, of course, is the Bosnian conflict.

Assumption of Humanitarian and Peacekeeping Responsibilities

The U.S. is an active participant in support of humanitarian relief operations and peacekeeping efforts. In addition to unilateral operations and support for U.N. actions, the U.S. has also supported and is involved with NATO activities in both these areas.

Lessons from the Gulf War

Observers have suggested several areas of lessons from the Gulf War. First, the Gulf War revealed gaps in the ability of the international community to detect Iraqi preparation of weapons of mass destruction, as well as the difficulty of detecting mobile missiles in wartime with current technology. Some critics have also suggested that the failure of the intelligence community to decisively forecast the Iraqi invasion of Kuwait also represents a flawed capability. U.S. officials and analysts have carefully reviewed the Gulf War for lessons which can be learned.

There is unanimous agreement that the conflict illustrated the importance of advanced technology for conveying data rapidly to the battlefield. Indeed, the Persian Gulf War highlighted the growing potential of advanced information technologies to obtain and convey battlefield and other tactical intelligence information in a timely manner to battlefield commanders and others in the direct theater of combat.

Thus, the Pentagon and strategic thinkers are seeking to anticipate the future battlefield and its military-technological implications. The term "revolution in military warfare" has been used to refer to advanced technologies and military systems which would enable the U.S. military to see the entire battlefield and use advanced weaponry, much more than manpower, in combat.

Among other things, as Rear Admiral Dennis Blair, U.S. Associate Director of Intelligence for Military Support has noted, "information from satellites. . .now can be spread around the world through satellites and fiber optic lines, so we can get the take from satellites out to tactical commanders."

Finally, a separate but related priority is "information warfare." This term has been used in different ways, but its most basic meaning concerns the development of capabilities to both protect U.S. communications from enemy attack, and also to possess the capability to degrade enemy communications and related activities.

End of Zero-Sum Game Approach

Because the Soviet Union posed a global threat, the U.S. tended to be concerned about external or even internal developments in almost any part of the globe and in almost any nation. This is because such developments in theory could have an impact upon the global struggle with Moscow by giving Moscow a geopolitical advantage.

Thus, for example, the Angolan civil war was perceived by the Reagan Administration as strategically important. It was believed that the triumph of forces aligned with the Soviet Union and Cuba could have given Moscow access to a key geographic point in Africa as well as to significant natural resources. With the end of the Cold War, however, developments related to many nations around the world no longer are a cause for great concern in Washington in terms of U.S. security interests.

Concerns About 'Rogue Nations'

Some nations, however, remain of great concern to the U.S. These include especially what have been termed 'rogue nations'; i.e. nations which, among other things: 1) maintain an ideological and political hostility towards the U.S.; 2) in general, are non-*status quo* oriented and which do not in practice accept the international rules of the game; and 3) either are interested in, or already in the process of, acquiring weapons of mass destruction (WMD), such as nuclear, chemical or biological weapons and the means to deliver them. Nations which would fit in these categories include Iraq, Iran and North Korea.

Proliferation Concerns

The potential for proliferation of both WMD and the means of delivering them (ballistic and cruise missiles etc.) has emerged as a major concern in the U.S. Indeed, if there is any one area of post-Cold War U.S. foreign policy consensus at present, it is that America should actively and vigorously seek to block WMD and delivery vehicle proliferation, especially in rogue nations.

Loosening of Export Controls

The end of the Cold War is resulting in significant changes in U.S. export control policy. The U.S. itself is loosening its export restrictions and has accepted similar changes in other nations. This is likely to increase the challenge to the intelligence community to detect and trace exports which are misrouted or re-transferred to non-eligible third parties.

Implementation of Arms Control Agreements

International agreements constraining or prohibiting the spread of WMD or their means of delivery have become a priority after the Cold War. In addition, the U.S. remains interested in pursuing or enforcing the more traditional conventional and nuclear weapon arms limitation pacts; this although the possibility of verifying some such agreements—such as for chemical weapons, remains a contentious political issue in the U.S.

Emergence of Trans-National International Challenges

Several less dramatic, but nonetheless important, international issues are receiving more attention from the U.S. after the Cold War although there is debate in the U.S. concerning whether such problems can legitimately be classified as security problems. These issues, sometimes referred to as 'trans-national issues', include the challenges posed by terrorism, organized crime and the narcotics traffic, as well as problems such as refugee flows. As Henry Kissinger has noted: "The problems of energy, resources, environment, population, the uses of space and the seas, now rank with military security, ideology and territorial rivalry...."

During the 1980s, a number of individuals on the liberal side of U.S. politics urged that the concept of U.S. national security should be expanded to include more than issues related to defense and military-related matters; some of these individuals later joined the Clinton Administration. With the end of the Cold War, these individuals argued, issues such as the environment, refugees flows and other such matters should be considered as national security issues, and therefore should receive some of the resources normally allocated to the military, and the defense and intelligence communities.

Increased Importance of Economic Policy Issues

With the end of the Cold War, international economic rivalries have emerged as a more visible issue. In addition, the Clinton Administration has deliberately racheted up the priority of U.S. international economic policy, and has demonstrated willingness to utilize governmental resources in a more vigorous and aggressive manner in pursuit of U.S. international economic objectives. There has also been developing a public and congressional perception that America's traditional allies are also economic competitors. Inevitably, without the galvanizing influence of the Soviet challenge, economic concerns have become a higher U.S. priority; the U.S. in general is becoming less willing to accept economic policies of its allies that it would have tolerated during the Cold War.

In addition, economic espionage against the U.S., even by friendly nations, has become a more visible concern. In the unclassified version of its first annual report to the Congress on this issue, the White House stated that "a number of countries pose various levels and types of threats to U.S. economic and technical information"; it added that many allies "target U.S. economic and technological information despite their friendly relations with the U.S." Reports also noted that Russia is still considered a major concern in this area. At the same time, the U.S. is also stepping up its efforts to monitor and otherwise observe economic-related activities of its traditional allies.

Other Important Factors Affecting Intelligence Policy

There are also several other important developments which inevitably will have an impact upon U.S. intelligence institutions and policies after the end of the Cold War. These include:

Domestic Focus and Budget Constraints

As has been widely noted, the general mood in the U.S. is inward-looking. There is a feeling that this is a time for addressing domestic concerns. A skeptical attitude towards the federal government has developed, along with a feeling among many Americans that its overall role should be reduced. The federal U.S. budget is being intensely reviewed for savings and in some cases entire departments are being targeted for elimination. Thus, it is not surprising that Senator Daniel Patrick Moynihan, a New York Democrat, recently suggested that the CIA as such should be eliminated (although he has apparently even more recently retracted that suggestion).

Impact of U.S. Political Culture

During the Cold War, the U.S. public and policymaking community conferred wide flexibility on U.S. intelligence community and in general tolerated extensive secrecy as U.S. intelligence assisted in struggle to contain and confront Soviet expansionism. At the same time, U.S. political culture has always been sympathetic to openness and instinctively suspicious of secrecy.

In addition, while over-generalizations should be avoided, it is fair to say that there exists a significant sector of the national media in the U.S. which is, in principle, skeptical about, or unconvinced of the need for many U.S. intelligence activities, as well as the secrecy that often surrounds them. Finally, there is much more willingness than in the past for government employees to either talk to the media, or to openly discuss or write about their current or past activities.

Geopolitics versus Morality in U.S. Policy

Most Americans have generally viewed foreign policy through a prism which includes moral issues and have felt uncomfortable with an amoral or cynical approach to international politics. This dimension of U.S. policy is deeply rooted in American history and culture and has been a factor in the conduct and critiques of U.S. intelligence policy.

This American tendency was greatly reinforced by the moral dimensions of the several decades long struggle between freedom and Soviet-driven Communist totalitarianism, and it helped justify the active U.S. efforts during the Cold War to encourage democracy and the protection of human rights in other nations.

The moralistic strain in U.S. thinking also affects the intelligence community very directly. Examples of the U.S. debate include whether assassinations should be prohibited at all times, the questioning by some Americans of U.S. involvement in the domestic affairs of other nations during the Cold War, and the recent criticisms of the CIA's occasional utilization of agents who themselves have been involved in morally questionable activities.

The New Republican Congressional Majority

The Republican majority generally supports an active U.S. international role (while cutting back in certain areas such as international economic assistance), and has sought to increase defense spending considerably over levels. In general, this new Republican majority has for the moment not made any wholesale reductions in intelligence community spending impossible.

Defusing of Foreign Policy Debate

During the Cold War, the existence of Soviet Communism had a polarizing effect on the debate over U.S. foreign policy. Those on the left viewed anti-Communists as obsessed with their anti-Communism, while those on the right believed that many on the left downplayed the threat from the Soviet Union and also minimized the negative impact of communism on nations where it had been imposed.

The CNN Factor

Americans, even those in senior government positions, are

now accustomed to obtaining information quickly and directly from distant locations via CNN television or other similar outlets. In addition, there are a plethora of publications providing intelligent analysis of important international problems. These realities inevitably place pressure on the intelligence community to provide services different from those readily available elsewhere, and information which also in effect reinforces the need for its existence.

Outlines of Future U.S. Intelligence Policy

The above historical, environmental and institutional factors will form a significant part of the framework within which post-Cold War U.S. intelligence policy will be developed. Given these realities, the outlines of likely U.S. intelligence policy can be discerned as follows:

• Because there is no consensus on the U.S. international role, and no clear national strategy defining U.S. national interests exists at this time, it will be correspondingly more difficult and challenging to develop and establish priorities for U.S. intelligence policy than during the Cold War era. In order to avoid unnecessary or wasteful activities, the intelligence community will have to work even more closely (including personal interaction, as opposed to one-way reports from the intelligence community to the policymaker) with the policymakers who are intelligence consumers.

• Since the potential threats to U.S. interests are more diffuse and fluid than during the Cold War, intelligence policy will have to be more flexible and adaptive than ever. Prediction of international developments is always challenging, but policymakers will want the intelligence community—whether via human intelligence or technology—to anticipate events such as the Iraqi attack on Kuwait.

•   With respect to individual nation intelligence priorities, the resource focus will likely be on: 1) Russia and China; 2) nations which may be in a position to affect the energy supplies of the U.S. or its friends; or 3) proliferation of weapons of mass destruction or their means of delivery.

•   Other intelligence priorities will include enhancing the ability of the U.S. to meet its various alliance commitments and responsibilities; this means, of course, U.S. intelligence support for NATO as well as the U.S. presence in Japan, and also for assuring that the U.S. can anticipate and, if necessary, respond to a North Korean attack upon the Republic of Korea. Indeed, the U.S. can perform a useful service to the extent it brings together intelligence officials from allies such as Japan and South Korea.

•   In terms of preparation for, and support of, actual military operations, the top priority will likely be low-to-mid-level conflicts ranging from a Bosnia to a Persian Gulf-type situation. Policymakers will thus need to define more clearly the division of labor on military-related matters between the CIA and the defense intelligence agencies, as well as restructure defense intelligence efforts as such.

It is likely that the military will be given more responsibility for battlefield-related intelligence. But the military will not be the exclusive agent for estimates of military capabilities of other nations, since the assumption of many policymakers is that the military tends to inflate such estimates.

In any event, U.S. intelligence efforts will be most effective when political and military objectives are clear. As the *Los Angeles Times* reported: "While Secretary of Defense William Perry has promised increased U.S. intelligence to help Western allies in Bosnia, officials and independent observers warned that U.S. measures will be hampered. . . by the lack of clear-cut policy or military objectives. . . ."

• The lessons learned from the Gulf conflict will result in a continuing effort to improve the translation of data gathered by advanced technology into immediately usable information that can support the U.S. battlefield forces, as well as to remain in the leading edge of information warfare capabilities. Of course, especially in view of the Ames spy case, traditional counter-intelligence will also have to receive renewed attention.

• Other battlefield-related intelligence capabilities will also be emphasized, including developing ways of detecting mobile missiles. In addition, it is likely that the current intense emphasis by the Congress and the U.S. armed forces on the minimization of U.S. military casualties, as well as civilian casualties, will result in an even greater effort to develop or deploy battlefield systems (including intelligence-related)—such as drone aircraft which are designed to accomplish this objective.

• Intelligence community support for U.S. involvement in peacekeeping and humanitarian-related activities will also continue to receive increased attention. While it is too soon for definitive lessons from the Bosnia experience, one conclusion that at least some observers have drawn from the U.S. involvement with the U.N. in both Somalia and Bosnia is that the U.S. needs to be more careful of the manner in which it shares intelligence information with U.N. agencies.

• The end of the global U.S.-Soviet struggle means that significant intelligence assets and resources no longer are likely to be allocated to monitoring or responding to developments in many parts of the globe which after the Cold War are of only marginal interest to the U.S.

• At the same time, there will be increasing resources and

efforts devoted to following developments in 'rogue nations';
perhaps over time, if such governments are viewed as a very
serious or direct threat to U.S. interests, U.S. policymakers may
direct active intelligence community efforts to counter or even
undermine such governments.

• Similarly, U.S. intelligence resources will be increasingly
shifted to detect, monitor and counter the proliferation of
weapons of mass destruction or their means of delivery, especially by (but by no means limited to) rogue nations and
groups.

• Also necessary will be an ability by the intelligence community to monitor or verify (to the maximum extent possible)
compliance with any international agreements constraining or
prohibiting the spread of weapons of mass destruction or their
means of delivery; and in addition, the U.S. will continue to
need a capability to verify more traditional arms treaties concerning conventional or nuclear arms.

• There are two areas which are likely to receive much
more intelligence community attention than during the Cold
War: first, trans-national issues such as terrorism, organized
crime and narcotics flows. These are important issues and
deserve high priority from the intelligence community.
Nonetheless, many Americans disagree with the attempt by
the Clinton Administration to include at least some of these
issues (for example, the environment) under the traditional
definition of national security. In any event, at least, in the
short run, the Clinton Administration's position has led the
intelligence community to place more emphasis on these non-
traditional areas.

The second area includes economic-related data and information (including learning what other nations are doing to
observe U.S. economic developments, and finding out what

developments are occurring elsewhere). Indeed, as the largest and most open economy which led in the establishment of international economic rules from Bretton Woods to GATT, the U.S. would naturally find it very important to utilize its intelligence resources to monitor compliance with these agreements. The U.S. has an obvious national interest in the observance of these pacts, especially since violations will inevitably undermine domestic U.S. support for its alliance relationships.

In addition, intelligence efforts on economic issues, while a fully legitimate function, will be somewhat contentious with America's allies, and the exact nature and degree of intelligence community involvement remains to be fully sorted out.

• Owing to budget constraints and a reduced U.S. international role, intelligence priorities will be given more intense scrutiny, and weighed more carefully against other needs than would have been the case during the Cold War. Under present plans, for example, there will be a reduction of 25% in intelligence community personnel during the 1990s. There will also likely be less redundancy in intelligence capabilities.

• Moral values and issues will continue to be a part of the context for the formulation and implementation of U.S. foreign policy. They will be particularly relevant to the intelligence community on issues such as whether the U.S. should encourage the building, or consolidation, of democracy and respect for human rights in other nations via intelligence community efforts (in addition to the overt and very public efforts of the U.S. National Endowment for Democracy).

What role moral issues and values will play in post-Cold War U.S. foreign policy remains unsettled, although their role will certainly be at least somewhat diminished without the existence of the Manichean struggle between right and wrong that the Cold War represented to most Americans. At a minimum, and especially after the Somalia imbroglio, it is unlikely that the U.S. will seek to utilize intelligence resources in broad so-called "nation-building" efforts.

CIA General Counsel Jeffrey Smith is developing guidelines on the question of CIA relationships with morally questionable agents. A *New York Times* editorial reports that under the new approach, "the agency's tolerance for misconduct would be governed by the value of the intelligence gained on a sliding scale in which every case would be decided on its own merits." Certainly, there is at least a minimal U.S. consensus that to the maximum extent possible the recruitment and use of agents abroad should be, as CIA Director John Deutch put it recently, "consistent with American interests and American values."

• Governmental secrecy has never been popular in the U.S. The direct and obvious threat to the U.S. from the Soviet Union during the Cold War somewhat neutralized the traditional American antipathy to secrecy, but the U.S. has now returned to a more typical situation where the burden of persuasion is upon those who would maintain secrecy in intelligence activities.

In addition, Americans place a high value on privacy. This is one reason the intelligence community is meeting resistance as it makes its case for limitations on computer software that make encryption difficult or impossible.

The absence of a serious visible threat to U.S. security will reinforce trends in the post-Cold War U.S. political culture that will create pressures to reduce or more carefully limit, regulate or otherwise constrain intelligence activities in general.

• The end of the Cold War has diminished at least for the short term some of the domestic polarization on foreign policy issues. With the domestic ideological and polarizing battles about Soviet Communism over, it is less likely that the CIA will either be demonized or defended uncritically. This may allow decisions on issues which were extremely contentious during the Cold War, such as the use of covert action by the CIA, to be made on a pragmatic basis.

Former Kennedy Administration official Roger Hilsman in *Foreign Affairs* argued that "covert political action is not only something the U.S. can do without in the post-Cold War world, it was something the U.S. could well have done without during the Cold War as well." This probably represents a last hurrah of the Cold War left-liberal approach to covert action.

Indeed, even the Clinton Administration is moving towards reinvigorating the covert action dimension of U.S. intelligence policy. In a September 12, 1995 speech, CIA Director John Deutch stated that "the U.S. needs to maintain, and perhaps even expand, covert action as a policy tool"; adding that such activities should have to be "approved at the highest levels of government" and include a "timely notification of appropriate Congressional oversight bodies." It is probable, however, that such covert actions will be used primarily with respect to rogue nations, and especially WMD and proliferation concerns, rather than, as during the Cold War, for efforts to affect the internal politics of a nation using such tools as propaganda.

• In general, the new Republican congressional majority will tend to be supportive of the intelligence community in terms of funding, as well as defending it from attack from those Americans who would like to see a significantly reduced U.S. intelligence capability and activities.

• The rapid availability of information from CNN and other media, as well as the wide availability of general information and analysis on international issues, will place increasing pressure on the intelligence community to make its information as user-friendly as possible, explain its views to a more questioning audience, and to perhaps even to withdraw from any responsibility for providing open-source information.

Conclusion

This is a challenging and crucial time for U.S. intelligence policy, and indeed for foreign policy in general; especially since this is the first period since the 1930s when the U.S. is not facing a direct and serious international threat. At the same time, there remain real international issues affecting U.S. national interests.

The fundamental issue, however, is clear. If the U.S. is to remain a global power and international leader, and maintain its alliances and other security commitments in the post-Cold War world, it will continue to require a robust intelligence capability, as well as sensible and effective intelligence policies for the new international era.

Thus, the challenge is to develop a coherent and sustainable policy in a time of relative normalcy that protects the interests of the U.S. and its allies in what is still a dangerous and unpredictable world.

In any event, even the best intelligence is not a panacea. In the majority of situations, there will probably be some ambiguity about such potential developments as the intentions of a potential aggressor before the actual moment of attack or the intentions of coup plotters before the actual implementation of the coup. Thus, ultimately, policymakers must themselves make key judgements and decisions; and policymakers and the public in a democratic society must not only correctly assess a situation, but must have the will to take necessary actions to protect their interests.

The future of U.S. intelligence in the American democratic system cannot be predicted. Unlike during the Cold War, the burden of persuasion will be much more on those who support an active and robust U.S. intelligence capability to explain and justify intelligence spending and activities; and any decisions, such as the elevation of CIA Director Deutch to Cabinet status, which appear to enhance the influence of the CIA will be subject to criticism.

However, having withstood vigorous attacks from critics during the Cold War, however, as well as more recent problems, the intelligence community is likely to remain, albeit with changes, a prominent and important dimension of U.S. international capabilities in the twenty-first century.

Chapter 5

An Israeli Perspective on Contemporary National Intelligence

Aviezer Yaari*

The post-Cold War era differs from the Cold War era in several important aspects.

The outstanding difference for the world, including the Middle East, is the easing of tensions between the superpowers, the United States and the former Soviet Union. In the Cold War era, the on going contest between the powers resulted in a rather mad arms race, in clearly defined battlefronts, and in keeping the Arab-Israeli conflict, amongst others, permanently alive. The new era brought certain changes: some moderation in

* **Aviezer Yaari** is Head of Defense and Security Department, State Comptroller's Office of Israel. He served as Commandant of the Israeli National Defense College and Deputy Director of Military Intelligence, the Israeli Defense Forces.

the arms race, and the opportunity for changing alliances and re-defining battlefronts. An excellent example is the forming of the coalition against Iraq in the Gulf War; another is the change in the atmosphere of the Arab-Israeli conflict, which has already yielded some very important developments in the 'peace process.' It is possible that these changes will create the foundation for even more spectacular developments, which will bring in their wake new intelligence needs and challenges.

So, with what problems is national intelligence faced? Which of the old problems remain relevant, which have become more acute, and which problems have newly emerged?

First, it is important to point out that the democratization process, which started after the end of the Cold War, has not yet reached the Middle East. The regimes' structures, established in the fifties and the seventies, in most cases remain stable;most do not show marked signs of positive development. Even worse is the continuing failure of most of the countries to absorb even a few democratic values to which they were exposed in the twenties to forties by the European imperial powers. Instead there has been a renewal of religious fundamentalist movements, to answer social and personal needs, while emphasizing the decay of the old "revolutionary" regimes. These movements pretend to employ democratic means in their fight against the regimes; in reality, they employ means parallel to terrorist activity. Regimes have turned into one-man dictatorships, relying on party or army bureaucracies; they no longer have any positive social or national context.

Next, it is important to mention that no disarmament process is taking place in the Middle East. Although the conventional arms race has slowed down somewhat, it has made way for the modernization of the armies, which have retained their influence. The freeing of available resources to social processes, which characterizes democratic or so-inclined, is prevented by the armies. In some states there is a marked escalation of arms race, expressed in their efforts to develop nonconventional weapons. To date, these efforts have yielded capabilities in chemical and biological warfare; unrelenting efforts are being made to reach nuclear capabilities. These efforts, together with the ability of authoritarian regimes to activate relatively big *regular* armies, create a constant threat. They have so far resulted in Persian Gulf wars: Iraq against Iran, and Iraq against Kuwait and the Coalition.

This combination of authoritarian states, fanatical terror groups and unconventional arms capabilities makes it strategically impossible for Israeli National Intelligence to relax or for the army to de-escalate readiness or preparedness for war. The threat range is wider today than ever. It spans from the threats of fanatical terror groups, with their simple and sophisticated weapons, to threats of modern conventional arms and the use of modern doctrines, to threats of use of weapons of mass destruction. Parallel to this heightened tension, strategic processes leading to reconciliation and even treaties of cooperation are unfolding in political and economic spheres, foremost of which is the Arab-Israeli peace process. There are those who go so far as to proclaim the advent of a new Middle East, where all will be conducted according to treaties and agreements instead of conflicts and wars. This vision has not yet materialized, but already it has set a new and important challenge for National Intelligence. The challenge is to understand the potential of the peace process towards regional development in economic and social processes, towards civil projects uncluding infrastructures for water, transportation and tourism, and towards making the most of each country's potential. Israel already acknowleges the need to prepare the field of intelligence for this new era, although it can not yet relax its vigilance as far as security is concerned.

Lessons from the Yom Kippur War

Israel, as well as other Middle Eastarn countries, considers the October 1973 War (Yom Kippur War) as the war which introduced new challenges to National Intelligence in the modern era. Even though it was a so-called "all-conventional" war, it was the first time where there was massive use of anti-aircraft ground to air missiles, and personal guided anti-tank missiles and even a first appearance, though not an impressive one, of theatre ballistic missiles of the FROG and SCUD varieties. On the Israeli side, the novelty was the use of the F-4 Phantom Aircraft which were set against the Mig 21 and 23. This was the first time, since Pearl Harbor, that a massive military-strategic surprise attack brought about a reassessment and a new awareness of intelligence.

This forum may be interested in the three main lessons learned:

First, the need for pluralism in the National Intelligence system;

Second, the need for long-term basic infra-structure research of the main processes that influence the trends towards either war or peace. This, **in addition to** strong and reliable day-to-day research to give a timely early warning;

Third, awareness of the danger of preconceptions in intelligence research. The Israeli Military Intelligence, in the October War of 1973, maintained an unwavering belief in the concept that war was not a practical option for the

Arabs at that time; of course this preconception was wrong.

Regarding pluralism, the idea is to establish parallel Intelligence analysis systems in the areas of military and political strategy. Ideally, they should have identical capabilities to work on the same pool of intelligence sources and to independently analyze the material before them. This way, the decision makers will enjoy a variety of evaluations concerning national issues and will be able to make more informed decisions.

Diverse intelligence services within one national framework is not an Israeli invention, nor is pluralism. However, a conscious effort has been made in Israel to establish pluralism and to break up the monopoly of a sometimes bureaucratic and authoritarian National Intelligence Organization(MOSSAD). Until now, success has been only partial. It seems that pluralism suits affluent nations more than it does poor ones.

As to the development of separate research entities-basic and current-within the National Intelligence Organization in Israel, steps have been taken but the goals have not yet been achieved. The ideal goals are specializing in current factual developments of the opponent's military, regime structure and economy and developing a good early warning system of war, revolution or an economic-social breakdown. This current intelligence is also the main support in crisis management. It is also important to develop a good *basic intelligence entity*, which should focus on the long-term development of infrastructures in the areas mentioned above in order to indicate significant 'basic' changes that occur within them. It should try to delineate potential indications of crises and opportunities, which have been noted in the fundamental processes. This 'basic intelligence entity' should also systematically study the personalities of antagonistic leaders. This is always an important aspect, especially in the Middle Eastern context, where the choice between extreme and moderate options often lies with one man. Thus it is crucial to try to fully understand the personalities involved. This basic research will supply added depth and more options in long-term national preparedness. In its purest form, basic intelligence entity also supplies the research on how the enemy evaluates us in order to give the decision makers the ability to balance development against development, or what is called net assessment.

Awareness of preconceptions in National Intelligence assessments became a major issue as a result of the October War. It is a most important issue in the methodology of National Assessment, which is rooted in the intelligence failure of that war. Even though there was full deployment of belligerent powers on the frontier, it was concluded that there was *no intention to attack* and that conclusion enhanced the surprise. In any conflict, especially when there is danger of war, one must prepare solely according to the enemy's capability and disregard any preconceptions. The rationale is that intentions-if we are aware of them-cannot be a good enough indication for what is to come, especially if we are dealing with dictatorial regimes, in which contrived deception is part of the military doctrine.

Actual preparations that demonstrate the capability of either side, expressed in the build-up of forces, their consolidation and finally their deployment in the field, allow a more judicious appraisal of possible options and decisions. If an enemy has gone into alert position, and one takes suitable and overt counter-measures, there is a fair chance that the enemy will withdraw. If the enemy does not withdraw, at least you are ready for whatever is to come. Not preparing oneself due to preconceptions of the enemy's intent is in itself a deciding factor for the enemy to attack.

This appears to be a useful enough concept and practical guideline, but mainly beneficial in times of crises, and then not always. First, it does not answer day to day needs, because its success depends on National Intelligence delivering an accurate description of the enemy's capabilities. This is not always possible. An excellent example of this in a global context is the progress made by Iraq in the area of nuclear arms, unknown before the Gulf War.

Second, a nation cannot always react to an opponent's capabilities without stretching its economic and national resources beyond their limits. The solution, then, is to take into account the opponents' intentions but to prepare against all eventualities according to the National Doctrine. This means that one has to assess the required minimum deployment in times when there seems to be no imminent danger of attack, and to be alert to changes in physical movement and concentration of forces of the opposing side and redeploy accordingly.

In Israel the people are all called to reserve duty in times of emergency because *they are* the army. In everyday routine the army is only a skeleton of a professional and regular army and carries the burden of preparedness for war. In other countries, where the army plays a more prominent role in keeping the regime stable, large regular forces are kept ready year-round, though distanced from its borders.

The supreme duty of National Intelligence is to define the elements which characterize the transition from peace to real tension and to sound the alarm in the event of such danger. We have experienced, more than once, how quickly peaceful conditions can turn into an emergency or even war. We hope that the peace process will eliminate this phenomenon from the agenda of the Middle East.

Lessons from Desert Storm

Next I would like to deal with the lessons learned from the
second Gulf War(Desert Storm). In that war we observed the
unfolding of technical potentials that constitute what is popu-
larly known in Israel as the *future battlefield* for the year 2000.
This includes;
- the capacity to aim and accurately hit strategic and tactical
  targets from afar
- the capabilities of deploying military forces 24 hours a day
  (due to advanced night-sight technology)
- the ability to take advantage of stealth technology to avoid
  radar detection
- the ability to employ Theatre Ballistic Missiles and Cruise
  Missiles.
- the flood of information.

In the spheres of intelligence we also include in SIGINT the
use of *airborne intelligence stations*(AWACS[1] and J-S TARS[2]) to
analyze, evaluate, inform and instruct big and diverse army
units during battle. All these, and other factors, brought about
the superiority of firepower over the element of maneuverabili-
ty on the battlefield. Nevertheless, those same factors, together
with modern logistics, enabled the side which had fire superiority to move its forces quickly and efficiently.

This war presented before the National Intelligence systems
of Israel and its neighbors a new agenda for consideration,
namely:

---

[1] Airborne Warning Control Aircraft.
[2] Joint Services Theatre Airborne Radar System.

- *Expanding ranges* of conventional wars and *reduction in warning time.*
- Involvement of an unconventional threat (chemical/biological) in a conventional war.
- Realization of the importance of Medium Range Ballistic Missiles in the modern conventional war.
- The required capability to analyze tremendous amounts of intelligence information in record time, and the ability to supply them on time to the armed forces.

Let us review this list backwards. National Intelligence should be organized so that it should be able to absorb all incoming information from various sources, to sieve it and extract what is relevant for Intelligence assessment and targeting. This begin with the National Intelligence Assessment and ends with the marking of precise targets for individual weapons. It requires reorganizing in such a way that computerized systems will replace the human eye and brain in absorbing the flow of information. The systems will make a primary selection, so that the expert will be able to better navigate through, instead of being submerged by, the abundant data and save his creative thinking for things that matter.

This raises quite a few problems, but let us now consider two which I deem to be important. The first problem is how to enable the technological brain of the computer to take over the thinking process so that it will be able to sieve though as many texts as possible, extract from them the necessary subject information while at the same time retaining important contents in case they were not spotted on the first run. It is the dynamic human brain which inserts itself into the computerized system by directing the process of sorting and storing useful information. From such storage it will be possible, later on, to create an intelligence evaluation that will lead to the interpretations and conclusions which comprise the Intelligence Assessment. This method is being re-modeled constantly, yet it is far from perfection and therefore will remain a challenge for future years.

The second problem is how to make the best use of overt and covert global data-bases, which are bursting with information. The approach should be either direct or through access of the data-flow channels. One theory, "Open Source Intelligence," is based on the awareness that **Internet,** and other similar networks, give National Intelligence access to global information pools. Theoretically this makes possible a more rapid, accurate, and complete collection of up-to-date data, which can be gathered openly from all over the global village instead of gathering individual bits of information from various sources, some covert, costly and slow. The same goes for screening secret system networks that Intelligence decides to pursue-but here as well, only a highly sophisticated computerized system will facilitate the realization of the tremendous potential.

Now let us consider ballistic missiles. There is a heated debate concerning their importance in the modern conventional war. There are those who maintain that as long as they are carrying conventional armament, ballistic missiles have no strategic advantage over aircraft; quite the opposite-what a bomber can achieve many times in many places, the ballistic missile can do only once, carrying only one tenth of the load and one-tenth of quality systems, and causing but one tenth of the damage. This is still being debated in Israel as a consequence of the Gulf War, in which some 40 SCUD missiles landed mostly in Israeli urban areas. I believe that military-strategic Intelligence should contend with ballistic missiles in trying to provide all information as to their whereabouts and their damage assessment. This is especially pertinent in the case of Israel, (and before that of Teheran) where ballistic missiles have penetrated, where previously aircraft had not, causing damage to property, mainly in populated areas. If the number of ballistic missiles increases to the hundreds, it will affect the national infrastructure with strategic consequences.

One must also take into account that when ballistic missiles gain precision and actually hit important targets, their effect will increase considerably. We should not be influenced by the overall scenario of the Gulf War, but should closely examine the details. American air supremacy was altogether so overwhelming; the air force could choose any target, destroying it with the help of air-to-ground missiles with even simply old-fashioned bombs.

The few ballistic missiles that did penetrate, to Israel and Saudi-Arabia, are the ones to warn us about future pitfalls.

Far more dangerous is the ballistic missile which carries a non-conventional warhead, of whatever variety. Here Intelligence should take accurate measures against each missile. This poses a new problem for National Intelligence in the Middle East, although it is old news for the superpowers. This problem needs to be solved by the next decade and therefore needs to be worked on immediately.

The same goes for the first issue mentioned: **The expansion in the theatres of war and the reduction in warning times,** again, thanks mainly to the ballistic missile. This is known to the superpowers, but new to us.

Today National Intelligence must provide an early enough warning, to enable preparation against aggression, from as far as 1000 km or more, as well as to give sufficient time for countermeasures to be taken in the few short minutes from the time of a missile launch to its arrival in our skies. This is also the time needed to warn the population. It is, for us, a new dimension to reckoned with, totally unknown up to the Gulf War, but apparently here to stay.

Modern Battlefield and National Intelligence

National Intelligence faces new problems concerning the modern battlefield. To some, especially those in the sphere of military strategy, no satisfactory solutions have been found. On the premises that conventional war with modern weaponry is the likeliest option, and especially in a region fraught with dangers and conflicts like the Middle East, one has to prepare by building a compatible new structure of forces with a newly organized and integrated Intelligence corp. It seems that this premise is valid for the Middle East as well as for many other areas of conflict around the world. The aspects to be considered in this context are:

1. The need for an Intelligence system which will meticulously scrutinize all sectors of the battlefield.
2. The need to supply accurate Targeting Intelligence in quick sequence.
3. The need to supply accurate *individual* Targeting Intelligence.
4. The function of Intelligence as a supporting system for continuous day-and-night fighting ability.

Regarding the need for an Intelligence 'scanner' to constantly and effectively comb every possible battlefield sector, this is a goal that suits the superpowers and they have made remarkable progress towards it. In the Middle East this is by now an acknowledged need, but its realization is a distant dream as of yet, it is doubtful whether within the framework of a single country a satisfactory answer will be found in the near future.

As already mentioned, the need comes from the risk of a surprise ballistic attack from great distance with a short warning time.

But the need is noticeable also in more traditional aspects of military threats. With improvements in military technologies and weaponry and resultant doctrines being developed, it will become possible to activate armies for a surprise attack on enemy lines or even behind them through deployment of forces in the strategic depth of one's territory. For example, commando forces, brought in by helicopters to a suitable site close to or even behind enemy lines, will lead the attack, while the main forces will be swiftly moved by air and motorized transport to the battleground. As you know, primary attempts to provide an answer to these difficult Intelligence problems in the spheres of satellite and U.A.V.[3] capabilities are also being made in Israel. But we are still far from happy with our achievements, especially in the face of mounting threats, as mouthed by the leaders of 'unstable' states.

To counter these incipient threats, technological answers are being developed. A very important one is the P.G.M.[4], the Tomahawk, or the M.L.R.S.[5], with its ability to hit precisely multiple targets and its longer shooting range. Their goal is to reach a "first shot-first hit" capability of a missile or shell, with the first hit being lethal. If that objective its achieved, there is a chance that expert activation of those weapons will lead to the swift destruction of multiple targets and so will render ineffective the performance of enemy forces *on the battlefield*. Moreover, an enemy whose forces are quickly and massively hit

---

[3] Unmanned Aerial Vehicle.
[4] Precision Guided Missiles.
[5] Multi Launcher Rocket System.

will fall more readily into disarray and conclude that the battle cannot be won. That is, of course, assuming there is somebody left to draw that conclusion.

Such a battlefield scenario could not be managed without Intelligence to supply the target information, which ought to be accurate enough to facilitate precise hits. Such information on stationary and mobile targets must be obtained to enhance strike efficiency and to exploit the potential of one's weapons.

The target information should reach the weapon in enough time for it to operate precisely, quickly, and for as long a time as possible. Many techniques are considered for use today regarding these demands; possible solutions are air reconnaissance, by a small U.A.V. connected directly to the individual weapon's system, airborne scanners in sophisticated intelligence aircraft, U.A.V. and satellites.

The last point I would like to make here is that to exploit fully the potential of modern arms and armies, one must provide them with the capability to carry out what is called 'Continual Fighting' This means exercising unrelenting, constant pressure on an adversary, denying him a redeployment line. To achieve this, night-vision techniques were developed, to allow unhindered flow of information on enemy troop movements, targets and terrain. This is another aspect where National Intelligence can either promote or hinder its success.

Problems of National Intelligence
in the Era of Peace Processes

It is important to phrase this heading precisely. We are talking about peace *proceedings* and not *established peace treaties*. This is the situation when we talk of the Middle East.

Therefore, as already stated, there exists the need to preserve the capabilities of National Intelligence in the spheres of military and political strategy. On the other hand, peace practices and experience are slowly being accumulated in the Israeli-Egyptian relationship and now in the Israeli-Jordanian relationship as well. Nothing, as yet, is firmly established and old problems still remain. But changes have occurred that call the attention of the Intelligence community to the requisites of the reconciliation era.

Three requirements which clearly call for immediate intelligence capability are:

1. Watchfulness for changes which may disrupt peace.
2. Intelligence in the economic-social sphere.
3. Intelligence on regional environmental problems.

There is no need to elaborate on the necessity of being watchful for any changes that may threaten peace, as we have already discussed that issue with "Non-Disarmament" in the Middle East. But it still must be made clear that in these matters, it is most important to develop sensibility to changes occurring in fundamental processes in the confrontational states, even though they may now be our partners in the peace process. To gain such sensibility one needs superb basic Intelligence research which will provide the means to form plausible suppositions on the future of regimes, their economies, and social struggles. Take for example fanatic Islamic forces on the rise in various places in the Middle East. Having observed past events in Iran and Sudan it should be quite clear how crucial it is for Intelligence to be timely and of good quality, especially in the case of a possible takeover of a secular state by fundamental forces. As far as Israel is concerned, this information is of the utmost importance, since the fanatic Islamic movement has taken a vow to bring about the destruction of the State of Israel. National Intelligence must specialize in studying such basic issues, together with academics whose area of expertise coincides with it. If anything of value is to be said in the context of Basic National Intelligence, it is the crucial integration of academic thinking with basic Intelligence research.

To this, in times of negotiations for peace and peace treaties, one must add the increasing importance of positive Intelligence in matters of national economy, national physical infrastructure, and environmental issues. It is likely that as soon as communication and cooperation between states is more firmly established, an entire section of National Intelligence will have to be reorganized. It will have to give answers to these elements which will need its expertise in order to enhance cooperation and understanding between the states. Government bodies, such as the Foreign Office, the Treasury, the Ministries of Transport, Tourism, Commerce etc. will be equal customers of that Intelligence. It may be that the same Intelligence, which contributed to the understanding of the conflict throughout the years when it was prevalent, will in the future contribute to its resolution, even at the cost of restructuring its military-strategic capacities. It is obvious, though, that intensive specialization within Intelligence is already needed for the peace process. National Intelligence, it would appear, needs to rethink its goals and to reorganize itself accordingly, in order to give reliable support to the budding cooperation processes, and to maintain its vigilance vis-a-vis potential dangers. Also, it is important to continue the dialogue with the academic world on areas of mutual interest *without* co-opting them into the Intelligence community, which should retain its independence and separate identity and functions.

Valid Classical Maxims in National Intelligence

Three classical issues, representing National Intelligence problems of old, are worthy of discussion. The debate over them is unending, as well as instructive. Based on experience gained contemporaneously, lessons for the future may be derived. One such issue is the need for HUMINT of high standard and historical depth, despite the fact that technological intelligence is continually taking over the functions of Intelligence.

The second issue is the continuing inability to supply solid predictions of future developments.

The third issue is the need for a better definition of the role of National Intelligence in the evaluation of national policy.

The best example to demonstrate the need for HUMINT, to complement SIGINT, is found in the development of nuclear and biological arms in Iraq. Apparently every known technical Intelligence device was used in Iraq, including Imaging. This can be deduced from the interest aroused since Iraq attacked Iran in September 1980. This was certainly true in 1990, when Sadam Hussein threatened to set fire to half of Israel and managed to conquer Kuwait. The vast majority of modern Western nations engaged themselves in a military campaign against that country, without really knowing its full non-conventional arms potential. It appears that there is no substitute to Human Intelligence despite its well-known weaknesses and the high price paid to activate it. Ignoring prewar suppositions, it is clear that the wide use of technological means proved insufficient to give a true picture. This was only achieved when a personal report revealed incriminating documents. When all is taken into account, without a human source, which provides a story or a document, there is no possibility for providing a well-founded intelligence analysis or picture. We are not speaking of all intelligence dilemmas, but only of those which necessitate a good feel for the situation in the field, the decisions and decision-making processes of leaders (especially at the strategic level), or penetration of technological know-how. Nations that did not take HUMINT seriously because it was not precise enough or not as productive as technological sources paid dearly for their mistake. The problem here is that the founding of HUMINT networks is a process which requires a lot of time and specific skills, both learned and bought. There is no way to rebuild it instantly, as when one decides to switch the focus of interest from one country to another, as so often happens all over the world today. Those who did not neglect this example of one of the 'oldest professions' go on enjoying its products while suffering the discomfort of dealing with its particular difficulties. Those who have neglected this particular asset have thereby altered the structure of their National Intelligence (in my opinion) negatively, even though they may have achieved wonders in the areas of Technological Intelligence.

It is fascinating to observe that throughout history, seers, oracles, diviners, palmists, coffee-readers, and astrologers have managed to foretell the future so much better than the best Intelligence agencies. They, of course, benefit from the fact that people tend to remember only their successes even if they had occurred by chance. Established Intelligence organizations, on the other hand, are mainly remembered for their failures. How many books have been written about Barbarossa, Pearl Harbor and the October War? Compare this to books of accomplished forecasting. How many professors have made a living out of Intelligence failures throughout history? It is a real treasure chest! But, one must admit there is a reason for this. It derives from the fact that until now, there is no reliable method of predictions of the future, nor is there a science of technological forecasting. Therefore, predictions in the sphere of National Security have yielded some extremely poor results as a basis for National Planning.

Because of that, and because National Intelligence has no option other than to lay before the leaders its assessment of expected and probable developments, one must find the solution within the boundary of uncertainty.

This simply means that National Intelligence should acknowledge its inability to predict, avoid trying it and instead simply assume that well-researched past and present might indicate various possible directions to future developments. Intelligence will assume that certain elements would be essential to facilitate those events, and it will formulate the possible directions for development as conceivable alternatives for the adversary to act upon.

When these alternatives are presented before the national leadership, they should be presented with reservations, as there may occur a break or shift in the familiar processes, whose dimensions, directions or results cannot be foreseen. There are other cases where a possible break may give some early indications and therefore could be roughly outlined, but are very rare indeed. However, when presenting possible assessed alternatives, Intelligence will qualify them by pointing out the measure of uncertainty with respect to each alternative. Finally, assisted by the state's planning authorities, Intelligence will try to describe to the leadership how one's *own* course of action may influence the probability of the adversary's reactions.

Lastly, it seems to me that quite often National Intelligence, as well as lower level Intelligence, err in performing their full and legitimate analytical role in national or other evaluations. National evaluation is the definition given to the decision-making process. Around the civilian leader's council table, as well as that of the military leader, the process of arriving at the most sensible decisions should be conducted by orderly consideration of all elements.

The **first stage** is to present for consideration the relevant intelligence on the subject under discussion; this means the relevant information on known facts and their interpretation. One goes on to define uncertainties or gaps in information, to qualify modes of operations available to the enemy and to evaluate any known information about enemy's intentions. Finally, an evaluation of probabilities as to modes of the adversary's future operations should be presented as well. After this first stage, the Intelligence team should refrain from proposing solutions or supporting any solution, determined at the council table, in order to remain objective. They may be asked to clarify particular issues, but they have to limit their answers to analysis and desist from taking part in the decision-making process.

According to procedures in many countries, when National Evaluation is completed, decisions are taken. Only then comes the very significant **second stage** of Intelligence work. It should consider the decisions taken as a starting point and a basis for a new situation, which will evolve when those decisions are implemented, then prepare a new analysis about possible consequences and developments and what it could mean in terms of the adversary's perceptions and operational alternatives for counteraction. With that done, Intelligence has fully accomplished its appointed role of National Evaluation in the decision-making process. There are cases where Intelligence did not carry out the second stage due to historical reasons and human weaknesses; the results were unfortunate.

A well-known example is the fiercely criticized war plans of Israel, prepared in 1973, which failed in the face of the Egyptian-Syrian surprise attack. The critics claimed that the Capabilities' Intelligence (to differentiate from the Intentions' Intelligence) which was supplied to the I.D.F.[6] was excellent, but that the counterstrike plans were faulty. When questioned if it made a new situation analysis after the counterstrike plans were formed, to evaluate the consequent meaning, effects and operational alternatives for the enemy, Intelligence admitted to the sin of omission. Thus, at that crucial time, Intelligence did not perform the second stage in the Situation Analysis procedure and did not present the leaders with the possible effects of their plans.

Conclusion

This chapter has attempted to present some of the problems faced by National Intelligence in the contemporary era as seen from an Israeli perspective. The Israeli case clearly illustrates that national intelligence is needed not only during the time of crisis, but also during the time of peace. It also offers us valuable lessons on the role of national intelligence in early warning, the importance of institutional pluralism in intelligence community, and proper conceptualization of national security agenda and intelligence assessment. Equally important is information and technology revolution and its impacts on the modernization of arms and weapon systems. National intelligence system should get out of the old inertia, and be prepared for new challenges posed by changes in arms and weapons sys-

---

[6] Israeli Defence Forces.

tems. Finally, preoccupation with technical intelligence should not overshadow human intelligence. Human intelligence is essential for obtaining finer pictures, which cannot be captured by technical intelligence, yet critical in arriving at accurate intelligence estimates.

Chapter 6

Redefining National Priorities and Intelligence in South Korea

Chung-in Moon*, In-Taek Hyun**
Woosang Kim***, Jung-hoon Lee****

National Security and National Intelligence: Analytical Considerations

During the Cold War era, one of the most important sub-fields of the international relations discipline was security

* **Chung-in Moon** is Professor of Political Science at Yonsei University and Executive Secretary of the Korean Society for the Study of National Intelligence.
** **In-Taek Hyun** is Assistant Professor of Political Science at Korea University. He was Senior Fellow of the Sejong Institute.
*** **Woosang Kim** is Associate Professor of Political Science at Sookmyung Women's University. He previously taught at Texas A&M University.
**** **Jung-hoon Lee** is Assistant Professor of International Relations at the Graduate School of International Relations, Yonsei University. He held teaching and research positions at the University of California at Berkeley and University of Tokyo.

studies as it pertained to a nation or a group of nations. For students of security studies, it was, in a sense, an age of "Renaissance."[1] The term national security, however, still remains somewhat ambiguous, its interpretation depending on the interpretor. Traditionally, national security was defined as the security of a nation against 'external' threats. In other words, it was the physical survival of a nation that was the most important aspect of national security. Lippman defines national security as a nation's ability to maintain its core values, even if this meant going to war.[2] Similarly, Wolfers defines the term as "the ability of a nation to deter an attack."[3]

Today, a much broader definition of national security is used, encompassing economic, diplomatic, and social dimensions, in addition to military and political dimensions. The objective of national security, therefore, is to protect and extend the core values of a nation against both internal, external, existing, and potential threats.

Three fundamental core values of a nation can be identified: 1) physical survival; 2) freedom; and 3) prosperity.[4] However, the simple protection and extension of these values per se cannot ensure national security. This is because some of the 'core values' can often be confused with the 'interests' of a ruling elite in a particular society. In an undemocratic political

[1] Stephen M. Walt, "The Renaissance of Security Studies," *International Studies Quarterly*, Vol. 35, 1991.

[2] Walter Lippman, *U.S. Foreign Policy: Shield of the Republic* (Boston: Little, Brown, 1943), p. 150.

[3] Arnold Wolfers, *Discord and Collaboration, Essays on International Politics* (Baltimore: Johns Hopkins University Press, 1962), p. 150.

[4] Daniel J. Kaufman, Jeffrey S. Mckitrick, and Thomas J. Leney, eds., *U.S. National Security* (Lexington, Massachusetts: Lexington Books, 1985), pp. 3-8.

setting, for instance, the goal of regime survival may take precedence over the goals and interests of the larger society. In such a setting, policies pursued in the name of national security may in fact prove to be harmful. Therefore, the question, 'who is in charge of national security in what kind of a domestic setting,' is very important in determining the true nature of national security. As such, it is safe to assume that the conduct of leaders in a democratic country is much more likely to serve the nation's interests, not their own.

If the main purpose of national security is to protect the core values of a society, where does this leave national intelligence? In other words, what is the nexus between national security and national intelligence? Generally speaking, intelligence is a product of "collation, evaluation, analysis, integration and interpretation of all collected information."[5] National intelligence, through its information gathering and analytical activities, is thus an important part of the process of national policy formulation for national security. To ensure the functioning of this mechanism, the intelligence community in South Korea is made up of various national agencies including the Agency for National Security Planning(ANSP), the National Defense Security Command(NDSC), and the Defense Intelligence Agency(DIA). Despite the agencies' sometimes overlapping activities and the inherent inter-agency rivalry, the ANSP has managed, as will be discussed in the following section, to maintain its primary role within the national intelligence community.

The intelligence production process entails four different

---

[5] Tyrus G. Fain, ed., *The Intelligence Community, Public Document Series* (New York: R. R. Bowker, 1977), p. 973; Amos A. Jordan and William J. Taylor, eds., *American National Security* (Baltimore and London: The Johns Hopkins University Press, 1981), p. 127.

stages. The first stage concerns the need for specific information from the intelligence consumers. The second stage is the collection of information by the intelligence community. The third stage is the analyzing process. Finally, the intelligence package is produced as appropriate. In this process, two aspects are of particular importance. One is the capability of the intelligence community. The other is the intention and will of the national leadership. Intentional or unintentional distortion of intelligence by the intelligence community or by the political leadership can potentially damage national security.

Against this background, South Korea, especially in the post-Cold War international context, needs to redefine its national security. With the relative reduction in the importance of military security, the scope of intelligence must become more diverse through various forms of renovation and restructuring.

In this light, the realm of national security and regime security should be more clearly distinguished. To this end, it must be accepted by the intelligence community itself that its primary objective is to enhance national security. With public awareness growing on such matters, this may be a natural, if not inevitable, development. Indeed, with democratization gradually taking root, there is a growing demand for the reduction of the role of the ANSP. In particular, the ANSP's continued involvement in personal surveillance and information collection for the purpose of regime security cannot be said to be constructive in a democratic setting.

Finally, selective opening of information and intelligence is needed to build national consensus. In the age of 'globali-zation' and 'democratization,' keeping a balance between the new demand for greater openness on the one hand, and the necessity to maintain traditional secrecy on the other, is one of the most important challenges facing the intelligence community in

South Korea.

National Intelligence in South Korea:
Historical Overview

In theory, the need for the establishment of a central intelligence service in South Korea arose, as was the case in the U.S., with a view to bolster national security through a variety of intelligence activities. The idea was to collect and analyze information, which would help the government formulate a sound policy, especially toward the communist North. Having relied solely on the U.S. for such services throughout the Syngman Rhee era, the task of creating South Korea's own intelligence agency was taken up almost immediately after the military coup in May 1961 headed by Park Chung Hee. In June, the Korean Central Intelligence Agency (KCIA) was brought into form under the directorship of Kim Jong Pil, then lieutenant colonel of the Army and one of the key members of the coup. Without proper guidelines, however, the new agency's operations quickly came to focus more on the security of the military regime rather than on that of the state. As pointed out by many, perhaps this was what the new leaders had in mind all along. Whatever the founding purpose, it is safe to surmise that with involvements in misinformation, appropriation of political funds, extortion, wiretapping, torture, administrative interferences, suppression of political opponents and student activists, the KCIA's indiscreet activities lent to its public image as a powerful and ruthless organization.

From the outset, the creators of the KCIA lacked a sense of the broader intelligence community and its role within it. Without a significant monitoring mechanism, important questions, among others, about the KCIA's overall competence, cost effectiveness and democratic accountability were never really considered in earnest. As such, the KCIA, with what amounted to a mandate from the top, tended to wield an inordinate amount of influence in shaping both the domestic and foreign policies of the military regime.

On the domestic front, the KCIA's implications in a number of government-related scandals contributed to growing public distrust. In particular, its role in what came to be known as the 'four big economic scandals' [sadae kyongjae hukmak]—manipulation of the stock market, illegal import of pinball machines, illicit disposition of imported sugar, flour, cement and automobile parts from Japan, and embezzlement of funds for the development of the Walker Hill resort—had the effect of consolidating its negative image.[6] This image worsened with the KCIA's continual meddling in politics, highlighted in August 1973, when Director Lee Hu-rak allegedly masterminded the kidnapping of opposition leader Kim Dae Jung from Tokyo. Rather than overseeing national security interests, the KCIA, through its involvement in such politically driven scandals, was readily identified as nothing more than a political instrument of the military leaders. In other words, the primary function of the KCIA was to make up for the regime's weaknesses, which arose from its lack of political legitimacy.

Similarly, the KCIA's role in the domain of foreign policy has also proven to be overbearing. Take, for example, the controversial diplomatic normalization talks between South Korea and Japan. The KCIA director's personal involvement in settling

---

[6] For an insightful account of some of these scandals, see Kim Hyong-uk and Pak Sa-wol, *Kim Hyong-uk jungon: Hyongmyong kwa usang* [Kim Hyong-uk's Testimony: Revolution and Idol](Philadelphia: 1982).

the compensation issue heightened the public's fears of unchecked collusion between the Park regime and the Japanese government that could possibly pave the way for Japan's "economic domination" of South Korea.[7] Fundamental to the public sentiment against the normalization talks-eventually leading to a pan-national opposition movement in 1964-was not whether the treaty should or should not be concluded, but rather the shrouded manner in which the talks were being handled by the head of a dubious agency. Another "foreign" policy area in which the KCIA has enjoyed the limelight is Seoul's policy toward North Korea. In line with the U.S.-China détente in the early 1970s, Director Lee Hu-rak made secret visits to North Korea, bringing about in July 1972 a joint communiqué calling for exchanges and peaceful unification. Although early hopes dissipated in the following year, the KCIA's direct role in this affair, arguably the most urgent of all South Korean policies, reaffirmed the agency's status as the most important and influential component of the government.

In sum, in spite of its motto, "Work in the shade, but head for a sunny place," the KCIA throughout the Park era could not undo the public perception that it was above the law, serving first and foremost the interests of the regime leaders. As correctly observed by the public, this sometimes meant going against larger national interests, as was the case in the South Korea-

---

[7] The Kim-Ohira Memorandum, as the agreement came to be known, settled the structure and the amount of the property claims amount. This was the result of a secretive meeting between South Korean KCIA Director Kim Jong Pil and Japanese Foreign Minister Ohira Masayoshi in October 1962. For further detail, see, for example, Lee Chae-o, *Hanil kwangyesa ui insik: Hanil hoedam kwa ku pandae undong* [Understanding the History of Korean-Japanese Relations: Korean-Japanese Talks and the Opposition] (Seoul: Hakminsa, 1984).

Japan normalization talks.

One of the great ironies of Park's political life is that in being assassinated by KCIA Director Kim Jae-kyu in October 1979, the organization that had so loyally served to protect and prolong his rule ended up being responsible—albeit inadvertently—for ending it. The circumstances notwithstanding, the fact that the KCIA director assassinated President Park put the agency to its greatest challenge since its creation nearly two decades earlier. For Chun Doo Hwan, head of the Defense Security Command, who aspired to take over the political leadership, the KCIA's "implication" in the assassination provided a convenient excuse to keep this once powerful organization in check. In fact, his Defense Security Command, having taken over the operational control of the KCIA, set out to restructure the agency, especially in two areas: 1) scaling down the operational scope; and 2) personnel change involving the eventual purging of some 300 operators. The process picked up momentum when Chun assumed directorship of the KCIA in April 1980, an act regarded as the final confirmation of his ascension as the paramount leader of South Korea. Following a tight enforcement of the martial law, a new constitution was written—partly in an effort to absorb the aftershock of the bloody clash between the military and the civilians in Kwangju in May— giving rise to the Fifth Republic with Chun nominated as the new president by the electoral college.

In a broader effort to redeem the new regime's tarnished public image, the KCIA's name was changed to the Agency for National Security Planning (ANSP) in December 1980. The symbolic change was meant to trigger a fresh start for the agency. In the same vein, Lho Shin-young, a civilian technocrat who had served as foreign minister, was appointed in June 1982 as the second ANSP Director. It was during this period that the ANSP began to quietly recover some of its lost influence. But, the real push to reestablish the agency into the political powerhouse it once was came with the appointment of Chun's closest confidant, Chang Se-dong, as ANSP director in the last phase of Chun's presidency. After presiding over the teacher's union strike, the incarceration of representative Yoo Sung-hwan, the torture and death of Park Jong-chul, etc., the ANSP, for better or for worse, was soon back in the political limelight. Although he had to step down due to the handling of the Park Jong-chul case, Chang helped return the agency to the earlier KCIA mold.

As will be discussed in the ensuing sections, the role of the ANSP has been the subject of continual debate in the post-Chun period at both public and governmental levels. One thing is for sure: with the maturing of democratic processes in a society that has long tolerated extensive abuses of power by the ruling elite, the ANSP will be hard pressed to exert the kind of power it once enjoyed in the not so distant past.

Post-Cold War, Democratization, and National Intelligence

As discussed above, intelligence in South Korea has served as an important political instrument, traditionally enjoyed by only a select few within the government. Up until the Roh Tae-woo administration, the necessary secrecy of the intelligence justified the centralization of power and authority. Intelligence was subject to neither legislative checks and balances nor public screening. Taking advantage of the legal and institutional shield of the National Security Law, the Anti-Communist Law, and the Military Secrecy Act, the South

South Korean government tightly controlled and manipulated the flow of information on national security and intelligence affairs. The production and dissemination of intelligence information has belonged exclusively to four organizations: the Agency for National Security Planning (ANSP), the Defense Security Command (DSC), the Defense Intelligence Agency (DIA) under the Ministry of Defense, and the Defense Intelligence Command (DIC).[8]

The dissolution of the bipolar Cold War system, coupled with the democratic transition and consolidation of domestic politics, since the latter part of the 1980s, has drastically altered the traditional concept of national security and intelligence. The advent of the post-Cold War order has not only realigned the overall security environment and threat structure, but it also called for a reconsideration of security postures involving threat perceptions, strategies and tactics, and intelligence information gathering. Democratization and the proliferation of contending interest groups in domestic politics have also influenced the restructuring of domestic parameters underlying national security management, such as ideology, institutions, and political structure.

Over the past several years, South Korea's regional security environment has undergone a profound transformation. Threat perceptions among regional actors have become very diluted. Taking advantage of the changing regional political situation, South Korea has undertaken 'Nordpolitik' to alter the security environment in the region. The move was designed to create a regional milieu conducive to tension reduction on the Korean

---

[8] Chung-in Moon, "Democratization, national security and civil-military relations: Analytical issues and the South Korean case," *Pacific Focus*, 5(1), 1989.

peninsula, as well as to open new horizons in the expansion of South Korea's economic relations with neighbors. South Korea has normalized its diplomatic ties with the former Soviet Union and the People's Republic of China.

These visible changes notwithstanding, many still find inter-Korean relations uncertain and precarious. North Korea is believed to have both the intention and capability to take hostile military actions against the South. The security decision-makers in the South argue that threats to national security will disappear only with the complete demise of the current Kim Jong-Il regime. They characterize inter-Korean relations as being in an uncertain stage of transition, in which conflict and peace are precariously interwoven.

Equally troublesome is an emerging threat perception, widely shared by South Korean leaders. The new perception is that even if threats from North Korea disappear, either through unification or other forms of political arrangements between Seoul and Pyongyang, the new security environment may not necessarily be favorable to the Korean peninsula. Three major actors in the region—China, Russia, and Japan—may pose new threats to a unified Korea.[9] Therefore, in the mind of South Korean security planners, military preparedness and security and intelligence services still make up the most important aspects of national survival. We cannot deny, however, that intelligence efforts, in the post-Cold War world have been reduced and are substantially different from those during the Cold War. Since the end of the Cold War, most of the security information that intelligence services had to seek

---

[9] Chung-in Moon and Seok-soo Lee, "The post-Cold War security agenda of Korea: inertia, new thinking, and assessments," *Pacific Review*, 8(1), 1995.

once with such effort is now freely available to the media, to academics and to diplomats.[10] Much of the strategic information on North Korea can be obtained easily through diplomatic channels, mass media, and other available sources.

While the end of the Cold War has made it much easier to gather security information on North Korea and other countries, democratization and changing domestic political parameters have influenced the reshaping of national security and intelligence machinery. National security policies no longer enjoy political insulation; an intelligence committee has been formed in the National Assembly to exert an important supervisory role. The National Assembly's oversight has substantially increased with the revival of a 'legislative audit' system. The resources and the potential political reaction to intelligence activities are thus subject to legislative review.

In addition, increased civilian participation in security decision-making is strongly advocated. With Kim Young Sam's civilian government, the Korean military has undergone immense internal changes. 'Hanahoi', the dominant military faction, has been removed from its central political position as a result of an extensive anti-corruption campaign that specifically targeted the military. The change has epitomized civilian control of national security, intelligence machinery, and the military. In February 1993, Kim Deok, a former professor of international politics, was appointed as the director of the ANSP, effectively placing the agency under civilian control.

Popular pressure has been on the rise for the amendment of the Military Secrecy Law, the dissolution of the Agency for National Security Planning, and a fundamental restructuring of

---

[10] See Colby's chapter in this volume.

the Defense Security Command, all of which were accused of having distorted national security information and of being instrumental in repressing civil society. The government has shown a receptive attitude toward these demands. While the Military Secrecy Law is being considered for limited amendment; the Defense Security Command has been substantially reduced in size and its functions restructured. The Agency for National Security Planning was also deprived of its right to engage in 'security audit' of government agencies. Furthermore, the Ministry of National Defense has begun to publish a white paper on national defense and to allow journalists more access to national security matters. With further democratization, the domain of national security is likely to be further politicized and bureaucratized, weakening its effectiveness, comprehensiveness, and flexibility. However, this restructuring process is expected to enhance accountability and responsibility of national security and intelligence activities. The remaining problem concerns the necessary secrecy of intelligence. Although members of the intelligence committee in the National Assembly are obligated to protect the secrets they learn during committee work, a national consensus-building effort is needed to answer the question of how to democratically control secret security and intelligence activities.

New Directions for Reform

As noted before, the national intelligence system in South Korea is facing the dual challenge of democratization on the one hand and a changing post-Cold War security environment on the other. The existing system may not be able to manage these challenges effectively, and incremental, if not revolutionary, reforms for national intelligence may be unavoidable. In this regard, several new directions can be suggested.

First, a more systemic linkage is needed between macro-level national policy and intelligence. Intelligence activities which are not grounded in firm and comprehensive national security needs can waste resources and time. It is essential for the South Korean government to craft a clear vision of national security and to set a new order of priorities of national interests.

National survival should still be the utmost national security priority, so national intelligence efforts should be geared toward this goal. In this regard, intelligence collection concerning early warning of potential or actual military threats from the North, military deterrence capabilities, changing regional security environment, and other strategic and military aspects are vital. As President Kim aptly emphasized in his recent visit to the new ANSP headquarters, the intelligence collection on North Korea should remain the top priority of South Korea's national intelligence system. This is precisely because of the precarious succession politics in the North and its implications for strategic instability on the Korean peninsula.

Preoccupation with North Korea, especially in military and strategic dimensions, should not, however, overshadow other aspects of national security which are gaining greater prominence in the post-Cold War context. Economic security, for instance, is becoming as important an issue as military security. Thus, promoting international competitiveness through a systematic collection and distribution of economic intelligence, especially in science and technology fields, while ensuring a stable supply of raw materials, seems an essential goal for national intelligence. Equally important is ecological security. Organic survival of a nation's population depends more on ecological factors, such as environment and epidemics (e.g., AIDS), than on external military threats. In addition, preserving social stability by eradicating the roots of social disorder—such as terrorism, organized crime, and drug use—constitutes an integral part of contemporary national security. The national intelligence system in South Korea, as such, should begin to pay more attention to these non-conventional security issues.

Second, the South Korean national intelligence system has been haunted by the ghosts of past authoritarian regimes. Political use of the national intelligence apparatus for regime security had the effect of not only crippling its original purposes and functions, but also severely undermining its legitimacy. Koreans automatically view national intelligence apparatus as a symbol of the abuse of public power, as an image of the Orwellian Big Brother, and even as a token of state terrorism. Such an image is an inevitable result of the failure to differentiate regime security from national security in utilizing national security organizations. Under past authoritarian rule, regime security was identified as national security, and loyalty to political leaders was an expression of patriotism.

In the brave new world of democratic consolidation and globalization, such practices will not only undermine regime security per se, but also threaten national security by fostering the dissolution of the national intelligence system, Thus, separating regime security from national security is the essential prerequisite for strengthening the national intelligence apparatus in South Korea. A recent amendment of the Agency for National Security Planning Act, which prohibits its interference in civilian politics as well as abolishes its entitlement to 'security audit' other government agencies, has offered an institutional and legal foundation for such a separation. This represents a positive development. One caveat is in order, however. Enhancing popular support for the ruling regime through effective and law-abiding management of the national intelligence apparatus should not be seen as the use of national intelligence agencies for regime security. Yet the current public mood appears to be against even such a logical application of governance. Thus, it is essential to devise a new institutional arrangement to reduce such public distrust.

The third element to consider in reforming the national intelligence system is related to the organizational structure of the national intelligence community. There are two interrelated issue in this regard. The first involves recent debates on the restructuring of the ANSP into two independent units: one devoted to foreign intelligence and the other to domestic security and counter-espionage, following the American model. In our opinion this could be counter-productive on several grounds—dilemmas of bureaucratic politics and coordination, institutional rigidity, limited effectiveness in coping with crisis situations, and resource wasting. As Oliver Williamson succinctly argues, cooperation and coordination within an internal organization are better than those between two or more different organizations. Moreover, newly emerging security concerns, such as economic intelligence, inflow of foreign drugs, and international networks of organized crime would require intimate and speedy cooperation between the two wings of national intelligence. Separating the two wings may make this difficult, thus undermining national security. The counter-productivity of such organizational reform is revealed by Russia's current dilemma with its intelligence affairs, which emanated from the disintegration of the KGB into several independent intelligence and security units.

The second issue involves the monopolistic position of the

ANSP in the national intelligence community. Indeed, the ANSP serves as the national intelligence organization. Other agencies, such as the intelligence wing of the national police, Defense Intelligence Agency, Defense Intelligence Command, Defense Security Command, and intelligence units of the National Unification Board and the Ministry of Foreign Affairs are minor, if not junior, actors in the community. Judging from the Israeli intelligence community's dismal failure in the wake of the Yom Kippur War, pluralism in the community seems desirable and even essential. In our opinion, however, the real issue at stake is not pluralism, but coordination. As for intelligence on North Korea and other foreign countries, a rigid compartmentalization among agencies has emerged as a major problem. On the other hand, excessive competition has become problematic in the areas of domestic security and counter-espionage. In order to minimize compartmentalization, overlapping, and unnecessary competition, there must be a comprehensive national intelligence coordination mechanism. In this regard, it seems worthwhile to establish a National Intelligence Council within the office of the president.

Fourth, there must be renewed efforts toward improving technical intelligence capabilities. At present, South Korea's intelligence collection relies primarily on human intelligence (HUMINT). As to technical intelligence involving imagery (e.g., military intelligence satellite), signal, and other non-imagery (e.g., COMINT, ELINT, FISINT, LASINT, RADINT, IRINT etc), South Korea has depended heavily on the U.S. perhaps with a partial exception of communication intelligence (COMINT). HUMINT is essential for detecting an enemy's intention, but insufficient in developing capabilities and deployment. Moreover, in the case of American disengagement from South Korea, the lack of technical intelligence capability could bring about devastating effects. Constructing technical intelligence infrastructure could be extremely expensive, but with the information and electronic revolution, readying for technical intelligence seems to be essential.

Fifth, it is near impossible to understand the internal workings of the national intelligence community in South Korea since public access to it is shut out. The intelligence community in South Korea appears to be preoccupied with day-to-day operations, while basic research, intelligence planning, intelligence estimates, and medium-to-long term forecasting have received much less attention. Several factors account for this trend. First is an institutional and organizational inertia built in by earlier intelligence officers who had either Japanese training or no training at all. As a matter of fact, the old KCIA represented an odd coupling of an American outfit (CIA) and the Japanese ethos (Nakano school). Second is the lack of resources for analysis. It is a well-known fact that the analytical bureau within the ANSP has not received the necessary funds to conduct basic research, necessary for long-term forecasting. Third, failure to recruit qualified employees hinders such research efforts. Finally, the absence of organic links between the intelligence community and the academic community serves as a major obstacle in improving basic research, intelligence estimates, and long-term forecasting.

Over the past few years, the ANSP has been making extraordinary efforts to strengthen its analytical/research functions. One such effort is the recent recruitment of advanced manpower (ph.Ds) of diverse backgrounds, including scientists and engineers. The establishment within the ANSP of the National Institute of Intelligence Training, which aims at both education and research, is another positive effort. Additionally, the ANSP has been forthcoming in opening dialogues with the scholarly community. We hope these efforts will facilitate the restructuring of basic research, intelligence planning, intelligence estimates, and long-term forecasting into a more comprehensive and systematic manner.

The sixth element of reform involves the social and political foundation of the national intelligence community. De-politicization of the intelligence apparatus is a cardinal principle. In order to ensure this, the national intelligence community should be able to build its own social constituents. At present, the public is hostile and at best neutral to the intelligence community. Such hostility and neutrality can serve as an effective deterrent to the politicization of intelligence apparatus, but they can also critically obstruct the normal function of the intelligence community. In order to alter the public mood, the national intelligence community needs to take on a more public-friendly attitude. This can be achieved through selective opening of information and more interactions with the civilian community. The transparency and accountability should be matched with the formation and expansion of its social constituents involving former members of the community, educators of national security issues, and other beneficiaries of the services rendered by the community. In this regard, recent workshops on organized crime, drug issues, and economic intelligence, all initiated by the ANSP, can be interpreted as positive signs.

Finally, in principle, the production of intelligence depends on the demands for intelligence. The ultimate consumer of national intelligence is the president. For this reason, his commitment to and effective utilization of national intelligence is essential for the development of the national intelligence community. This requires a re-evaluation of the national intelligence agencies by none other than the president himself.

Chapter 7

National Intelligence in Japan:
Myth and Reality

Akio Kasai*

Introduction

Chances of occurrence of a war on the worldwide scale receded on account of the end of the Cold War between the East and the West. Meanwhile, there are gradual emergence and aggravation of various conflicts caused by religious, ethnic, territorial or economic discords, which had been long contained under the East-West confrontation. Although the international society is continuously striving for a more stable order than ever, future prospects of such an attempt seem to be obscure and there has been no clear-cut direction yet. It is said that intel-

---

* **Akio Kasai** is an advisor to Itochu Corporation. He served as a senior official at the Japanese Cabinet Intelligence and Research Office.

ligence agencies in each of leading countries are currently reex-
amining their organizations and activities preparatory to new
developments after the Cold War.

However, in the Asian and Pacific area, vestiges of the Cold
War remain as unresolved issues over the Korean Peninsula, the
Spratly Islands and Japan's Northern Territories. Due to such
the circumstances, the end of the Cold War does not directly
give an intensive impact enough to press Japan's intelligence
agencies to review their organizations and activities drastically.
It is true, though, that there are renewed voices arising from different circles to call for reevaluation or reexamination of Japan's
intelligence system and of the way that intelligence agencies
should be; these voices came out of lively debates on the growing importance of Japan's role in the international society and
on the crisis management system that was questioned by the
great earthquake and incident of sarin poisoning.

The Economist magazine of the United Kingdom launched a
harsh criticism as follows: "major changes are on the way for
Japan's security system: just about everything to do with security, from spying to dealing with disasters, is coming under scrutiny:" and "Japan lacks capability for full-scale intelligence."

The U.S. *Time* magazine formerly released a cover story,
which featured ranks of intelligence agencies in the world, cat-
egorizing them into four grades, and gave a high appraisal of
the second grade to Japan's most representative intelligence
agency, the Cabinet Intelligence Research Office (CIRO).
However, currently, the magazine also severely criticizes
Japan as "it is far behind the other developed countries in this
field."

Intelligence agencies in any country, more or less, live in the
realm of myth and their real images are befogged. Japan's intelligence agencies, which had been long mythified, are now seek-

ing ways to rearrange the communication network for intelligence and to strengthen their connection with departments taking charge of policy-making, in response to a demand from the real world.

This paper is a rough sketch to brief the readers on the present situation of Japan's intelligence community. It should be beforehand emphasized here that all description, including opinions, in this paper is nothing other than a private view of the author of this paper.

Japan's Intelligence Community

Intelligence Community

Japan's Intelligence community is a compound flexibly connected among five administrative organizations, which carry out intelligence activities on the nationwide scale respectively: the Cabinet Intelligence Research Office (CIRO), the National Police Agency (NPA), the Defense Agency, the Public Security Investigation Agency (PSIA) and the Ministry of Foreign Affairs (MOFA). These organizations engage in making intelligence reports in obedience to their respective responsibilities for businesses, through collecting and sorting out open and covert information and materials on foreign and domestic affairs, and in addition, analyzing, evaluating and examining them.

The Joint Intelligence Committee has been set up for the purpose of synthetic grasp of information, which these five independent government organizations preserve respectively, and with the aim of contacts about and coordination among policies launched by them. The committee is chaired by the director-general of the CIRO and held with the presence of the committee members who rank as director-generals in charge in the respective agencies. The vice secretary-general of the Cabinet Secretariat also attends the committee, as well as the director-general of the Cabinet Security Affairs Office.

Central Intelligence Machinery—Cabinet Intelligence Research Office (CIRO)

Organization

The CIRO is the only intelligence apparatus inside the Cabinet Secretariat. Under the direct instruction of the prime minister and the secretary-general of the Cabinet Secretariat, the CIRO is headed by its director-general, with departments of administration, domestic, foreign and economic affairs and documents and data processing. The staffs are comprised of intelligence experts from various fields and officials seconded for the CIRO from the ministries and agencies concerned.

Duties

The CIRO is in charge of business regarding collection, analysis and investigation of information with relation to important policies of the Cabinet. The scope of CIRO's intelligence targets covers all administrative areas, such as internal, international, political, economic and diplomatic affairs, security and public safety.

The CIRO's director-general shall straightforward make a report to the prime minister and the secretary-general of the Cabinet Secretariat more than once a week. The CIRO always retains its communication network in case of emergency and gives notice of sudden momentous issues occuring inside and outside the country to both the premier and the secretary-general of the Cabinet Secretariat without delay.

The Cabinet Secretariat, meanwhile, is authorized to coordinate among administrative departments, and the CIRO consequently plays a liaison role on important policies for the Cabinet, in regard to intelligence matters. Such a role specifically contains collection and assessment of intelligence-information and management and direction of the intelligence community or agencies.

Other Intelligence Apparatus

National Police Agency (NPA)

The NPA is in charge of maintaining public safety and order, and carries out its duties of counterintelligence and counter-terrorism, as well as makes investigation on, cracks down and takes preventive measures against crimes. In case of a disaster such as a great earthquake, the NPA also devotes itself to emergency operations, that is, collection of information on damages, on-the-scene guiding for evacuees and rescue activities. Since the NPA mandate overspreads the whole public security administration, the scope of its target information ranges widely.

Defense Agency

The Defense Agency serves for the purpose to safeguard Japan's national independence and security and engages in collection and assessment of military intelligence-information regarding defense of the national land.

Public Security Investigation Agency (PSIA)

The PSIA is in charge of control of assemblages conducting mobbish sabotages continuously or repeatedly and investigates such destructionist groups apart from the police. It has no authority to search.

Ministry of Foreign Affairs (MOFA)

The MOFA conducts analysis and assessment of the international situation, through centripetally grasping information collected by Japan's diplomatic corps during primary activities on diplomatic affairs.

Background of Reevaluation of Intelligence Activities

Features during the Cold War

Compared with Japan's national power and its international responsibilities, its intelligence agencies are extremely small on their respective scales. There has not been yet a large-scale central intelligence agency as the U.S. and Russia maintain. Additionally, the relationship is vague between intelligence agencies and other ministries and agencies promoting their respective policies, and it can never be said that the significance of intelligence-information, as a whole, had been highly recognized and appraised throughout the national policies.

This year just marks the 50th anniversary of the end of World War II. After that war, Japan renounced war and has pursued nation-building under the national policy to be an economic power. During the Cold War period, Japan was put in an unstable position in the international circumstances; however, it could survive without being involved in warfare, entrusting its national security to the Japan-U.S. alliance. There used to be lively activities by foreign intelligence agencies toward or within Japan in the period of severe East-West confrontation; thus, Japan's machinery bearing responsibility for counterintelligence has been well-organized earlier in the period and has continued its duties.

On the other hand, a general information-collecting agency was barely established at the time that Japan became independent after it had concluded peace with Allies. This agency has been developed into today's CIRO. However, the Japanese government did not have much understanding toward the significance of intelligence, and government sensitivity to foreign intelligence likely had tended to be blunt as well. This was because Japan had consistently kept a modest diplomatic attitude as a member of the Western bloc in the rooted Cold War structure. Moreover, the intelligence authorities of Japan in war played a role to restrain the people from enjoying their rights and freedom, in order to consolidate an order supporting war. Because of this history, the Japanese people have a strongly cautionary view toward intelligence agencies and stubbornly resist against rearranging and strengthening them. Since the above condition, reviews and rearrangement of Japan's intelligence agencies have been long left untouched.

In the meantime, the CIRO, in spite of its small capacity, has enjoyed a certain appreciation of its intelligence activities in specific fields, such as intelligence on political and military developments in Japan's neighboring countries which had belonged to the Eastern bloc. Other intelligence agencies in Japan can be said to have stood comparison with the CIRO, achieving some results in their respective fields.

Details of Review and Reappraisal

In response to the weakened East-West confrontation and the intensified nature of diversification in international society, Japan, more than ever, has been demanded to contribute to the international community. Besides, national interests became complicated among countries in the international situation after the Cold War and, as a matter of course, there have been also growing voices requiring Japan's own intelligence-information.

The Provisional Council for the Promotion of Administrative Reform (RCPAR), which was set up by the government to reorganize and promote efficiency of the administrative bodies, spelled out current requirements for Japan to contribute to and play an appropriate role in the new international order after the Cold War, in proportion as the promotion of its international position, and to ensure a harmony with the international society. Lively arguments in the RCPAR were thus further continued, being drawn from experience during the Gulf War. In October 1993, the PCPAR finally submitted the findings of the council to the prime minister, recommending to strengthen diplomatic functions, especially the intelligence-gathering system, and to take necessary measures so that the government can make decisions and actions swiftly and with mobility, under unpredictability of the current international circumstances. In other words, the PCPAR emphasized that it is important in the unpredictable and complexed international situation for the Japanese government to make an expeditious decision regarding each international situation. The PCPAR added that Japan's administrative mechanism which used to rely on a procedure of the bottom-up policy-making cannot respond adequately under such circumstances any more. The RCPAR then called for the prime minister, as the chief of the Cabinet, to exert his strong leadership and urged to enrich organizations to support himself.

In August 1993, the MOFA implemented a large-scale reform of its organizations and newly established the Intelligence and Analysis Bureau, taking into consideration a course of discussions in the PCPAR. This newly established Intelligence and Analysis Bureau appeared with the purpose of promoting the ministry's intelligence routine efficiently. The MOFA rendered the bureau to specialize in intelligence, after its predecessor, the Information and Research Bureau, detached functions for developing policies and ensuring comprehensive national security from itself and left a function of collection and analysis of information only to its business; the former functions were transferred to other bureaus.

Meanwhile, the Defense Agency has considered to reorganize and unify its inner apparati being in charge of collection and analysis of international information on military affairs, which existed in the Ground, Marine and Air Self-Defense Forces respectively, into a central intelligence office inside the Joint Staff Council since some time before. In August this year, the agency officially determined this reorganization as a policy for the coming fiscal years. The establishment of such a central intelligence office means that a new organization will be born to enable for the agency to collect and analyze wide ranging intelligence-information on regional disputes in the world and military postures of other countries, as well as terrorism, disasters and peace-keeping operations.

It can be said that each intelligence agency is at last starting a step-by-step review of the organization, paying a bill which

was run up by that Japan had put independent efforts for collection and analysis of information on the back burner under
the Cold War structure.

In the meantime, the Great Hanshin Earthquake that hit
Kobe in January this year caused devastating damage in the
amount of 10 trillion Japanese yen and 300 thousand victims,
five thousand deaths, and led to destruction of the urban infrastructure, such as a highway networks, and port and industrial
facilities. In March, a cult named *Aum Shinrikyo* carried out an
unprecedented heinous crime by scattering poisonous gas-
sarin-in the subway in Japan's capital, Tokyo, giving rise to over
5,500 injured.

The government had had a blank for nearly half of the day
till it had taken emergency action during the Great Hanshin
Earthquake, such as the dispatch of the Self-Defense Forces
and emergency goods, due to a delay of reports about the
earthquake. The government was hence subjected to harsh
criticism insisting that a number of causalities were brought
by a man-made disaster. Similarly with the sarin case, since
the same type of the gas was used in a former case in a local
city during the previous year, there also appeared strong criticism condemning the entire lack of any specific warnings or
relief measures and accusing the government's total unpre-
paredness for emergency reaction against sarin-used terrorism
as an oversight.

In relation with the government reactions toward the above
two cases, serious debates on national crisis management in
various circles. Voices were increasingly raised here again to
demand revision and reexamination of Japan's intelligence system and agencies from various viewpoints.

It may be possible to say, based on views of the unpredictability of international circumstances by the collapse of the

Cold War framework, Japan's growing responsibility in the international society and reconstruction of its system for the national crisis control, that there is a broad understanding on the significance of intelligence and a pressing demand to take specific measures swiftly.

Current Measures for Reform

The following three points can be summarized on the basis of most of hitherto discussions and measures, as regards rearrangement and consolidation of the government intelligence functions. Each of them is about management of the Cabinet Intelligence Research Office (CIRO).

Strengthening the Emergency Function for Concentration of Information

In addition to quality, information can be meaningful only when they are conveyed to the scene for examining policies at the right time and used for proper decision-making.

It is impossible for the government to overcome a crisis, which is within a category of emergencies such as the sarin poisoning and the Great Hanshin Earthquake, unless a flow of information is guaranteed for expeditious reports and orders between on-the-spot staffs and the prime minister as the supreme leader. During the Great Hanshin Earthquake, it cannot be denied that there were some delay of a flow of emergency information within the government, though the local governor's function as the field control tower was temporarily paralyzed. Organized rescue activities were then lagged from the outset.

Based on such reflection, necessary amendments of laws have been made in order that the government can swiftly take countermeasures through its leadership in case of emergency. At the same time, authentic information should be sent to the prime minister without delay, as a prerequisite for his exercising strong leadership. A decision was recently made to assign the CIRO, which is under the direct control of the prime minister, to play a role as a control center for information regarding such emergency cases. It has thus become clear that the CIRO plays roles of a receiver and sender for all the information concerned, as the Cabinet's hub of information. Since this clarification, integration of information channels were attained between the Cabinet, as the supreme organ for decision-making in the administration, and each administrative department. Moreover, it will become easy to rearrange the order required for reports and contacts. It will be possible hereafter for the government as a whole to tackle a crisis with mobility more than ever.

Since such a function of the CIRO as a hub of information should also work at peacetime as a matter of course, it is expected that the function will be useful for smooth flow of information among the government departments.

In the meantime, preparations are under way to build a new Prime Minister's Official Residence (PMOR), setting five years later as the target year for the completion of construction. The control room for the supreme command is due to be annexed to the new PMOR, and the CIRO is currently considered to undertake management of the control room.

Enrichment of the Joint Intelligence Committee

While timely conveyance of information is important, it is needless to say that contents of information should be good enough to contribute to on-target judgements for policy-making. At present, each intelligence agency acts independently. However, with consolidation of mutual cooperation and connection among the intelligence agencies and coordination among objectives and contents of their respective activities for intelligence, Japan's intelligence community as a whole may achieve effective results with more steadiness than ever. For this reason, it is expected that some measures should be taken, including a drastic review and reorganization of functions of the Joint Intelligence Committee and coordination among policies and priorities of the respective intelligence agencies, stepping into each agency's information-gathering activities. It will be difficult, though, to materialize these measures immediately under the present situation, due to each original role of the intelligence agencies. Accordingly, it is desirable to assess achievements of the respective agencies properly, to make competitive relationships and stimulate among the agencies and to seek a way to enrich intelligence activities as the whole intelligence community more than before. In any case, coordination among and activation of the whole intelligence community are currently taken into consideration through upgrading the status of the CIRO's director-general who presides over the Joint Intelligence Committee. This step seems to be crystalized soon.

Consolidation of the Link between Intelligence and Policies

The CIRO used to limit extremely its contacts for reports.
This is based on a policy as the CIRO bears a primary obligation
to make reports to the prime minister and the secretary-general
of the Cabinet Secretariat, and at the same time, on a view of
preservation of intelligence confidentiality. However, it is
required and proper for the policy-making process to notify the
final decision-maker, as a matter of course, and moreover, the
responsible policy-makers of intelligence-information with
adopting measures to preserve secrecy of intelligence. It should
be strictly banned that an intelligence officer insert his own
intention or prejudice regarding a specific policy into any stages
of the intelligence cycle, such as collection and assessment of
intelligence-information. Insofar as this is taken into account, it
is preferable that intelligence and policies should be separated
and each of them should be independent. In this sense, it was
meaningful that the MOFA made the Intelligence and Analysis
Bureau independent.

Based on the above conditions, intelligence-information
itself can fulfill its primary mission only when it is used for the
policy-making process. One example for a linkage between
intelligence and policies could be shown in the presence of the
director-general of the Cabinet Security Affairs Office at the
Joint Intelligence Committee. It is expected, furthermore, to
make intelligence reports to, not only the ministers of state who
are members of the Security Council of Japan, but also the
responsible policy-makers of the ministries and agencies concerned at the proper time, and to keep a close connection
between intelligence and policies. On this point, the initiative of
the CIRO as the central intelligence apparatus is expected to be

exerted actively.

Conclusion

There is no argument, for the time being, to seek a drastic reform such as aiming at new establishment of a large-scale central intelligence organization or total revision of the current Cabinet system, although rearrangement and consolidation of Japan's intelligence community, or its agencies, has been surely required. Japan is sometimes taunted for being a country with small intelligence notwithstanding an economic giant. However, an intelligence agency can show its real value, when the agency is indeed operated under a decisive will of the nation on the basis of the support of its people. The current review of the intelligence agencies has been done within matters of management on the beaten track. It could be said, though, as a progress above all things for activities of Japan's intelligence agencies that the significance of intelligence has been widely understood inside and outside the government. At all events, it is a right course for Japan, under better consideration, to make modest but steadfast progress in rearranging the intelligence community, while Japan should maintain broad relationships for cooperation with friendly and allied countries and ensure its national security in the international society.

Chapter 8

Economic Espionage and Counter-Espionage in the United States:
Threat and Policy Response

William T. Warner*

Introduction[1]

In July 1995, President Clinton attempted yet another resolution of the intense five-year debate over the scope—if any—
and methods associated with officially-sanctioned gathering of
economic information from foreign businesses and governments. This debate has involved two administrations (Bush and

---

* **William T. Warner** is an attorney and a former U.S. naval intelligence
officer. He has written extensively on economic and technology espionage.

[1] Portions of this chapter have been excerpted from the author's article,
"International Technology Transfer and Economic Espionage," which
appeared in the *International Journal of Intelligence and Counterintelligence*, Vol.
7, No. 2 (Summer 1994), pp. 143-160.

Clinton), the Congress, the U.S. Intelligence Community (some-times referred to in this paper as the "IC," or the "USIC")—including three CIA Directors, and U.S. business leaders and organizations.

As this chapter amply documents, there is no question that the U.S. industrial technology, including the U.S. defense tech-nology, has been and is being increasingly targeted by foreign governments and their agents and surrogates.[2] Not unexpected-ly, this development generated an immediate public consensus within the U.S. to have the government mount defensive responses. But the matter of a "tit-for-tat" policy directed toward the U.S. engaging in state-sponsored industrial espi-onage has been quite controversial and has not in fact been implemented.

The President has reportedly[3] issued a directive to the Director of Central Intelligence, the nominal head of the com-bined U.S. military and civilian intelligence community, which for the first time explicitly calls for the CIA—supported by all other IC agencies and bureaus—to assign a high priority to what the President designates as "economic intelligence."

While the exact terms of President Clinton's directive are classified and thus not directly available for analysis, enough is known about the new policy to be able to spell out with some

---

[2] The paper discusses two broad factors which make an exact measure-ment of the extent of foreign penetration of U.S. industry extremely difficult, if not altogether impossible. One factor is the lack of a universally accepted and employed set of definitions which apply to the area of "economic intelli-gence" and "economic espionage." The second factor, which is to some extent, tied to the first, is the lack of reliable data on the extent of foreign activity in this area.

[3] "Clinton Reportedly Orders CIA to Focus on Trade Espionage," in *The New York Times* (Supplement), July 25, 1995, p. A-38.

precision what is involved.

Aside from policy questions about economic espion-age/intelligence, the health and performance of the U.S. econo-my has been the focus of the Clinton Administration even before it came into office in January 1993. International competi-tiveness and so-called "fair-trade" issues have clearly dominat-ed this Administration's agenda because of the President's core belief that these areas hold the key to the success of the U.S. industry, thus resulting in domestic prosperity, including increased jobs.

Viewed in this context, the recent policy directive is both consistent with overall Administration goals and a logical out-growth of the implementation of those goals.[4] In addition to maintaining a strong defensive posture against foreign state-sponsored economic espionage, the new Clinton policy report-edly takes the USIC into some quite controversial new areas involving pro-active, covert intelligence operations such as fer-reting out negotiating positions of adversaries in sensitive trade talks, and monitoring foreign-government compliance with trade agreements.[5]

The new directive also orders the USIC to step up an appar-

---

[4] In a related development which is probably connected to the President's new economic intelligence initiative, current CIA Director (and DCI) John M. Deutch recently announced that, after years in the policy "dog-house," covert action is being revived as an essential instrument of the U.S. intelligence operations; see "Expansion of Covert Action Eyed," in *The Washington Post*, September 13, 1995.

[5] One of these operations mounted by the CIA and the State Department, whose purpose was to glean secret French negotiating parame-ters in the 1993 GATT talks, blew with an embarrassing public bang when a French counterintelligence operation caught and expelled five U.S. embassy personnel; see "France, in Apparent Espionage Spat, Asks Five Americans to Leave Country," in *The Wall Street Journal*, February 23, 1995, p. A10.

ently successful existing effort which involves using the National Security Agency, as well as other IC agencies, to monitor commercial bribery, and other sharp practices which tend to place U.S. corporations at a disadvantage when competing for foreign contracts.

The questions this chapter will undertake to address are, first, whether or not this particular policy pronouncement has in fact satisfactorily settled the debates and controversies which have focused on policy issues relating to economic espionage[6]; and, second, whether or not the policy— including its omissions—holds any promise of dealing meaningfully with the challenges posed by the "New World Order" in the economic and technological, as well as the diplomatic and political arenas.

An informed assessment of these kinds of questions requires a detailed understanding of the why, the what, and the how of foreign economic espionage against U.S. industrial technology in the post-Cold War environment; that is, why U.S. industry is increasingly targeted, what specific technologies and processes are vulnerable, and how the theft of critical technolo-

---

[6] The term "economic espionage" is used rather than the more familiar "industrial espionage" because it is broader, and more descriptive of modern economic rivalry and conflict between nations. In the contemporary global economy, having information about a secret government trade initiative, or a confidential marketing decision made by a private company, can be as valuable as a proprietary formula or process. The term also helps distinguish traditional strategic geopolitical or military espionage which explicitly targets a nation's capabilities and intentions to wage war. That kind of distinction is of course blurred by at least two factors relevant to this analysis: first, political/military strategy nearly always has an economic dimension; and, second, a great deal of modern high-end, "cutting edge" technology, such as microprocessing and integrated circuitry, is essential both to state-of-the-art defense industrial base and to a competitive commercial economic sector.

gy is attempted and accomplished.

The chapter will also examine the state-sponsored or state-sanctioned economic espionage activities of two particularly aggressive foreign intelligence agencies, the Russian [formerly Soviet] KGB/GRU, and the French DGSE.[7]

Finally, the chapter will review deterrent and remedial efforts undertaken by the U.S. government and industry to counter economic espionage: foreign and domestic counterintelligence operations, export controls, and enhanced private industrial security.

Background

Since at least the early 1930's, and probably before, the former Soviet Union maintained a massive effort to obtain U.S. and Western industrial technology by any means it could—by exploiting military assistance from the Western powers [including Germany] before and during World War II; by wholesale appropriation of factories, technicians, and scientists from occupied territories after that War; by classic espionage methods, including clandestine purchases to avoid trade embargoes; and, during cyclical relaxation of tensions, by using normal commercial international trade channels.[8]

---

[7] Post-Union Russia and France are by no means the only major players in the 1990s economic espionage game. CIA Director Robert Gates has told Congress that as many as twenty nations are currently involved in government-sponsored clandestine intelligence operations which target U.S. industrial secrets; see [Gertz:1992c] These nations include [in addition to Russia and France] Japan, Israel, China, Egypt, Korea, Argentina, and even the United Kingdom. [Waller:1992; Schweizer:1993]

[8] In the interests of balance, it should be pointed out that the U.S. was

Before and during the Cold War, the former Soviet Union sought technology in support of its drive to build rapidly and to sustain a modern industrial base and very large strategic military forces capable of countering the Peoples Republic of China and the Western Powers.

The Soviet push to obtain U.S./Western technology by any and all means, including espionage, continued unabated through the Gorbachev era of Glasnost and Perestroika, and has actually escalated sharply as the Soviet economy continues to unravel.[9]

After the collapse of the Union in 1991, the Russian Republic "inherited" nearly all the Soviet foreign and domestic intelligence and KGB/GRU security apparat.[10] While these

---

just as aggressive in obtaining intelligence on Soviet weapons and technology by means of espionage and covert action. [Weber:1994]

[9] An extended analysis of the existing Russian economy, or that of the former Soviet Union, is not within the scope of this Memorandum, but three basic points are to be made about the centrality of economics to that society: first, the Russian economy—never really healthy—continues to be whipsawed and savaged by the stresses and contradictions of attempted conversion from command management to a free market system; see, e.g., my (1991); second, the imperative of dealing with the economy as a matter of national survival, is not only a political black hole for leaders and policies, but also a kind of singularity from which everything else in and about that society demonstrably flows; see my (1992a); and, third, the first and second points are the most important circumstances which propel the current Russian drive to obtain the U.S./Western technology.

[10] Under the old Soviet Union, the KGB, or Committee on State Security, had both domestic and foreign jurisdiction, roughly analogous to a combination of the CIA and the FBI in the U.S. The KGB has purportedly undergone a recent reorganization to split up these and other functions. Whether this has actually happened, however, is disputed even by Russian observers; see p. 9, n. 18, below.

The GRU was, under the Union, and still is, the primary military intelli

organizations are now freed from pervasive Party control, they nevertheless continue an aggressive agenda of economic espionage against U.S. and Western technology.

On the economic side, high-end U.S./Western technology is now sought as an important means of delivering the Russian economy from terminal disintegration. On the military side, purloined technology also supports an economic objective. It is a matter of dispute whether or not foreign technology is now devoted to outgunning the West, but it is certain that advanced technology is being applied to upgrade the technical sophistication of key weapons systems in order to facilitate sales in the international arms marketplace which earn critically needed foreign exchange.[11]

While France is not in the same dire economic straits as Russia, state-sponsored economic espionage serves generally the same ends: maintaining the technological competitiveness of its industrial base, and obtaining critical miliary technology.

As in the Russian case, French economic espionage follows a corporatist pattern of promoting government economic, trade or military policy. The DGSE conducts clandestine operations to acquire the needed information, and turns it over to one or more of the many industries in which the French Government has a financial interest or which Government pol-

---

gence service, supporting the Ministry of Defense and the missions of the military forces. In its organization, it is roughly equivalent to an amalgam of the U.S. Defense Intelligence Agency and the intelligence branches of the separate armed services.

Both the KGB and the GRU have been, and are presently, heavily involved in economic espionage.

[11] The persistent and steep decline of Russian oil and gas production has left international weapons sales as the only substantial prospect for significant export earnings. See p. 10, below; see also my (1991).

icy favors.[12]

The U.S. as a Target of Opportunity

With the strategic military confrontation which characterized the Cold War substantially abated, if not altogether ended,
there has been a worldwide revival of the traditional mercan-
tilist notion that economic power is the fundamental component of national power. An obvious corollary is that economic
information propagates economic power.[13] Both the U.S. private
industry and the U.S. Government are apparently coming
around to an awareness that the achievement and maintenance
of economic power is a matter for intelligence concern as well
as traditional fiscal policy. [Munroe:1992; Boren:1992;
Carver:1990][14] Even the OSD/JCS "Net Assessment" of poten-

---

[12] Ever the practitioners of realpolitik, the French spy without discrimi-
nation on allies and enemies alike. Targets include companies in which the
French Government has a financial interest, either directly or indirectly
through friendly "investors." Many authorities believe, moreover, that DGSE
penetration strategy often involves buying an interest in targeted multina-
tionals for the express purpose of looting its technology for Government purposes. See, e.g., Ewell (1992), Gertz (1992a), and NSI (1992b).

[13] A number of intelligence experts and scholars, such as Angelo
Codevilla, disagree that commerce equates to war in terms of national
power and national security. [Ewell:1992] Codevilla, and others, argue that
obtaining industrial secrets—whether business plans or technology—doesn't
necessarily translate into commercial success or advantage. It is crucial not
only to produce, but to do so competitively, in short: to master all the inter-
locking components of the free market, particularly "how the competition
thinks." Codevilla says a viable national market economy". . . invent[s]
things faster than people can steal them."[Ewell:1992]

[14] But the degree of government mobilization is quite controversial, and
is still unresolved in the U.S. Wright [1991:204-206] argues that corporatist

tially hostile foreign military capabilities now looks hard at the broad national economic factors which are likely to spawn the technology necessary to produce and maintain advanced weapons [Holzer and Leopold:1992].

The end of the Cold War not only changed the game, it shuffled the players around. Last year's political/military ally is now this year's economic antagonist.[15] This is not really surprising because the existence of a thriving world market economy with strong, independent—even predatory—competitors is the direct result of U.S. liberal internationalist economic policies during the Cold war.

U.S. economic globalism has not only internationalized American business methods and processes, it has showcased American technology. Everybody wants it and tries to get it one way or the other. Most nations—friend or foe—have either used American technology as a springboard to development [France, Japan, e.g.], or become "hooked" on it for their very survival [the former USSR].

------

economic management practiced by states such as Japan, Britain, France, and [the former] USSR involves". . . martial[ing] the full assets of their governments, including intelligence assets, to support their economic vitality," and that espionage and intelligence collection are the "primary tools" in the economic portfolios of these nations. He submits that nations such as the U.S., where the promotion of commerce is essentially a private function, are structurally restrained and inhibited in this kind of competition. Codevilla and others would disagree; see n.12, above. It could also be logically argued that President Clinton's July 1995 directive on economic intelligence moves the U.S. in the same direction.

[15] Porteous [1993:4] argues that the so-called "realignment of adversaries" also strains traditional intelligence-sharing networks, which in turn jeopardizes the kind of cooperation necessary to other key security areas such as anti-terrorist and counter-proliferation initiatives.

In addition to the quality and utility of U.S. technology, there are two additional factors which make the U.S. an appealing target for economic espionage, one technical, and one social and political.

The technical factor involves those aspects of the so-called electronic "information revolution" which have digitalized information generation, storage, transfer, and reception while drastically reducing the size, cost, and operational complexity of equipment used to control and manage data. [NSI:1992c] When secrets were recorded on documents locked away in safes, stealing information relied upon classic espionage techniques: physical theft of actual plans or documents, bribing or compromising individuals in possession of the desired knowledge, or other techniques which risk "leaving tracks" and ultimate detection. Stealing information in the "digital age," however, can be accomplished merely by intercepting formatted data at some point, either where it is stored, or as it is transmitted. The same technology which has made possible the development of digital information management has also bred relatively surreptitious systems of electronic snooping: unauthorized penetration of protected databases, illegal interception of digitalized transmission signals [which NSA does legally], and other methods.[16]

As U.S. business relies more and more on electronic information management, it renders its secrets more vulnerable to electronic theft.[17]

---

[16] Unless sophisticated and expensive countermeasures are in effect, most illegal data interception leaves no tracks. Even when it does, the identity of the spy is almost impossible to determine. [Ewell:1992; NSI:1992d; Lee:1993]

[17] An obvious and increasingly available way to thwart digital data interception is to encrypt, or code the data at its source, with the "key" for deciphering the code given only to authorized recipients. The U.S. law

The social and political factor which makes the U.S an inviting target for economic espionage is the openness of its society, and the relatively non-coercive character of its political institutions. [Wright:1991] A mass of commercial and technical information is routinely published and otherwise available on virtually any subject of interest to a foreign entity.[18] Where the specific facts are not published in detail, the likely source of the information is.[19]

An open society such as the U.S. not only provides more opportunity for getting information through open sources, it provides superb cover for clandestine or illegal activities contrived to steal restricted data, particularly from private businesses which rarely have sophisticated defensive measures in place. [NSI:1992a] Further, civil liberties under the U.S. constitutional system, particularly the presumption of innocence, as well as the absence of a centralized investigative and law enforcement authority, unquestionably inhibits totally effective apprehension of spies.[20]

----

enforcement and intelligence agencies generally oppose the unrestricted dissemination of this technology to the private sector, and are seeking legislation regulating its use, because it could also be used to conceal criminal activity. [Markoff:1992] Government regulated encryption is extremely controversial, and has been vigorously opposed on both technical and civil liberties grounds. [Sussman:1994]

[18] Governmental officials concerned with critical technology leakage occasionally challenge the ingrained culture of virtually unrestrained technology accessibility by attempting to stem the proliferation of "open source" academic and professional output—with little or no success. [Beardsley: 1985]

[19] In other words, for instance, a careful and regular reader of, say, *The Wall Street Journal and Aviation Week* may not be able to pick up the precise details of proprietary trade or technological secrets, but he/she would know who had the secrets and where to get them.

What Are They After?

During the height of the Cold War, the intelligence agencies of the USSR and those of its client states primarily targeted U.S. technology for the purpose of upgrading its weaponry, including high-performance microchips and supercomputers, and integrated circuits and minicomputers. [Melvern, et al:1984:16-17][21] The aim was not only to reduce the cost of weapons development but to eliminate research and development lead time so that new and upgraded weapons could be rapidly deployed. Other significant target technologies were optics, missile guidance systems, radar and sonar, nuclear reactors, aviation propulsion, and machine tools.[22]

------

[20] This is of course a deliberate political choice reflective of historic American values which render suspect unchecked centralized governmental power of any kind. Although, arguably, this arrangement makes U.S. society more vulnerable to spies, most Americans believe the cure—a KGB-like organization or a relaxation of civil liberties—would be worse than the disease, and too high a cost. Foreigners see American preference for domestic liberty at the expense of national security as foolishness, a virtual invitation to espionage. [Melville:1985; Reibstein, et al:1991] Domestic critics bemoan the comparatively [vis a vis, say, France] lax and uncoordinated U.S. counterintelligence response to its distinctive status as an appealing target for economic espionage. [e.g., Wright:1991] Most of these critics exhibit little understanding either of the underlying historic political roots of U.S. counterintelligence development, or of the social and political trade-offs which would be necessary to make spycatching more "effective."[Fort:1993]

[21] Tuck [1993:3-4ff] argues that nearly all key Soviet and Warsaw Pact weapons systems literally "ran on" Western-primarily U.S.-technology.

[22] Various Soviet collection agencies and bureaus actually generated written "shopping lists." In May 1980, the FBI seized and searched the briefcase of Andre DeGeyter who was a Belgian national and an accused Soviet

Computer technology was [and is] not only critically important to the operation and performance of state-of-the-art weapons systems, but also to their design and production. The Soviets quickly learned and understood that the same level of computer technology was also essential to the production of capital goods necessary to sustain a modern industrial base— for civilian as well as military production. [Melvern, et al:1984:17ff] U.S. technology was sought by the Soviets not only to build weapons but to prop up their perennially sagging domestic economy. [Melvern, et al:1984:73; Newport:1985; Hanson:1987; Seib:1992a; Tuck:1993]

Even with the Cold War ostensibly over, economic spying directed by Russia [and other former Union republics] has increased significantly. [Gates:1992; Chuah-Eoan:1990][23] Because

---

spy. Among DeGeyter's papers was a "shopping list" of high-tech items desired by the Soviets which included specialized programming language used by missile control systems. [Melvern, et al:1984] In 1985, The West German secret service recovered a thick catalogue called the "Red Book" which was identified as a copy of the official KGB high-tech "shopping list." [Kapstein:1985]

[23] Zagorin(1992) discusses the proposition that reports of increased KGB economic spying have been inflated by the CIA and other Western intelligence agencies who are looking for useful work in the post-Cold War era. Most writers, including Zagorin, discount such claims as Russian disinformation [see, e.g., Wright:1991 and Ewell:1992]. Zagorin's article cites the 1992 arrest and conviction, in Belgium, of a Belgian "journalist" who was credentialed to cover U.S. Shuttle launches, but who admitted to spying for the SVR [Russian Foreign Intelligence Service] as recently as January 1992. SVR is supposedly a spinoff of the "reorganized" KGB, but it is most likely just the same old KGB First Chief Directorate, doing business as usual under a new name. [Za]oga:1992; Waller:1992] One quite authoritative report has the KGB conducting economic espionage through its SVR "front"for the benefit of other CIS Republics. [Rahr:1992]

Most observers believe that KGB "reorganization" under Gorbachev,

of the interchangeability of modern industrial technology between "civilian" and "military" applications, it is difficult to classify what the Russians are after in those precise terms, but the main effort is clearly to provide a life ring to a struggling economy. As in the past, the most critical specific need is to implant stolen technology where Russian industry cannot afford to invest in research and development.[24]

---

and in the wake of the August 1991 coup, exists mainly on paper except with respect to the non-Russian Republics who got rid of the KGB root and branch. [Kalugin:1992; Waller:1992; Rahr:1992; Seib:1992a] Key legislative enactments and decrees necessary to implement the "reorganization" have been repeatedly rescinded or shelved. [Waller:1992; Zaloga:1992]

[24] In 1991, the last year of the Union, the Russian Republic comprised 76% of the USSR landmass, 51% of its population, and 61% of its gross domestic product ["GDP"]. By the end of calendar 1992, the Russian [Republic] economy will have shrunk to three-fourths of its 1989 level. Worse, the annual rate of GDP decline is actually increasing, from a -4% in 1990 to a projected -16% to -18% in 1993. By the end of 1993, Russian GDP is expected to bottom out at approximately 60% of the 1989 level. [Hanson:1992; Bush:1992]

While Russian export earnings are perking along at an estimated 1992 annual rate of US$30 billion, there was a net trade balance deficit of US$2.3 billion in the first quarter of 1992 caused primarily by the virtual abandonment of import controls which had been pinching domestic production. By way of comparison, Russia had a net trade surplus of US$40 billion in 1989.

As of April 1992, Russian gold and hard currency reserves were reportedly down to 170 tons of gold, worth approximately US$2 billion, but only US$60 million in convertible currencies. Western-style capital flight is an emerging problem because of [apparently] uncontrollable government spending, and high inflation caused in significant part by the failure to stabilize the ruble. Proposed levels of loans and credits from the IMF, World Bank, and G-7 nations [US$24 billion] will not significantly ease shortages of capital for domestic investment because of the lack of central fiscal discipline. [Hanson:1992] Virtually the entire Western financial assistance package—and more—will almost surely be required for servicing Russia's share

The Russian defense industry has fallen on equally hard times with production down as much as 50~75% or more in some sectors [such as shipbuliding], but it is still trying to maintain extensive research and development in high-tech areas with primarily military objectives such as combat fighter aircraft, nuclear weapons, and rocket propulsion. [Foye and Clarke:1992b:42, "Parliamentarian criticizes Defense Spending"] Whether the objectives of this kind of development are military and strategic, or purely economic, or both, is the subject of continuing intelligence and policy debate. [See, e.g., Boren:1992] That controversy notwithstanding, foreign arms sales were always a staple of Union exports, and it is clear that the current Russian government—not unlike most Western Governments—views competitive success in the international arms market as a palliative for internal economic problems. U.S. and Western technology has long been, and is currently the key to the Russian Defense Industry's ability to compete. [Dudney:1985; Hanson:1987][25]

[US$40 billion] of the former Union's convertible currency debt which comes due in 1995. [Bush:1992]

Serious capital shortages, caused in substantial measure by declining export earnings, adversely impact production levels of those very industries—such as oil production, aerospace, and heavy machinery—which provide 90% of Russian hard currency export sales. There is simply no money to invest in maintenance and improvement of plant and equipment, or in research and development. [Bush:1992;Knecht:1992]

[25] Both the Russian Republic and the former USSR have long led the world in foreign arms sales, but there has been comparatively little domestic economic benefit. This is illustrated by the fact that in 1990, of over US$14 billion in arms "sales," only US$4 billion was "in cash" [hard currency or barter], with the rest going for soft currency, "loans," or assistance credits to "ideological friends." [Bush:1992]

Military equipment remains virtually the only Russian commodity for which there is a foreign market. Expanded hard currency export earnings for

The Soviet program to develop a supersonic passenger transport ["SST"] ahead of the U.S. Boeing SST, which was canceled, and ahead of the British-French Concorde, which is still in service, was based almost entirely on technology theft. It was only Party interference and managerial blundering that caused the Soviet SST Program to fail. [Moon:1989][26]

The French Government sustains an equally aggressive program of economic espionage, aimed at much of the same

---

domestic investment—including defense conversion—is still the primary goal of arms sales [Foye and Clarke:1992a:27, "Russian Effort To Sell Arms in Middle East"; Foye and Clarke:1992b:39, "Arms Sales To Finance Conversion"]

There are numerous reports and other indicators that the "hightech" end of the Russian defense industry has been exempted from "swords to plowshares" conversion and directed to proceed apace with the development of new and improved weapons systems. [See, e.g., Foye and Clarke:1992c:70, "Conversion in the Aerospace Industry"; and Hanson:1992] The Mikoyan Design Bureau, for instance, has an advanced version of the MiG-29 [designated the MiG-33] in flight test.[Aviation Week 6-22-92] The advanced version reportedly incorporates state-of-the-art digital cockpit technology, upgraded weapons system computers, new airframe production techniques, and an improved aerodynamic design-all on the KGB high-tech "wish list."

[26] The French were of course major targets for Soviet SST espionage, and Moon relates several accounts (1989:99, e.g) of how French counterintelligence detected and "turned" Soviet agents, and reportedly used them to feed false plans and data to the Tupelov Bureau which was designing the Soviet SST.

Moon's superb book also relates in fine detail how stolen technology is integrated into the Soviet [Russian] design/production process—which, he concludes, is often problematic. Lacking the advanced materials and production tools and techniques used by the West, Soviet designers had to improvise and substitute. In a curious way, Moon argues, the result was in fact a uniquely Russian product, an amalgam of Western ideas and Soviet adaptation, not necessarily the exact copy of the Concorde dubbed the "Concordski" by the Western media.

U.S. technology which is of such compelling interest to the KGB/SVR—computers, aerospace, and production tools and processes. The DGSE specialty is infiltrating spies into the U.S. and foreign offices of high-tech U.S. multinational corporations such as IBM and Texas Instrument. [Ewell:1992; Reibstein, et al:1991; Ignatius:1992] Stolen secrets are then passed to French-owned corporations. [NSI:1992c; Schweizer:1993:96ff][27]

Hard technology acquisition is not the exclusive object of economic espionage. The lifeblood of the modern global economy is a complex network of proprietary and often confidential trade data, investment information, bids for contracts, commodity pricing, and market data. [Ewell:1992; NSI:1992d; Seib:1992b] Theft or leakage of this type of information can be as damaging to the victim company or nation as loss of a unique design or process, and as beneficial to the thief.[28]

How Do They Do It?

Economic espionage is a function of economic intelligence, but not all economic intelligence-gathering involves clandestine, often illegal, practices such as espionage. Nearly all major international corporate players pursue "competitive intelligence" or "strategic analysis." They glean massive amounts of

---

[27] Nations other than Russia, France, and Japan [including Yugoslavia] are reportedly after—in addition to computer and optical technology—food-processing technology, pharmaceutical formulae, telecommunication, even marketing techniques. [Gertz:1992a; Schweizer;1993]

[28] As noted above, p. 6, the digital technology used to maintain and transmit this kind of information actually facilitates its interception and theft. See also NSI (1992b).

information on competitors and relevant market conditions from public sources and subject it to sophisticated, often computerized, extrapolation and analysis. [Ewell:1992; Munroe:1992; Waller:1992][29] The Japanese Secret [Intelligence] Service, working with the Ministry of International Trade and Industry ["MITI"] are the acknowledged international masters of the art of government-sponsored competitive intelligence. [Ewell:1992; Gertz:1992b; Schweizer:1993:66ff and 127ff]

The Soviet government, Japanese and French corporations, and occasionally U.S. defense contractors have used the technique of "disinformation" to frustrate competitors. [Gertz:1992a; Clark and Griffiths:1986] "Disinformation" is the proverbial false brail. Deliberately sham or spurious or misleading commercial or technical information is circulated to the press, or introduced or offered in a manner likely to be picked up and relied upon by the desired target[s]. The problem with this ploy is the so-called "blowback effect": the possibility that the disinformation will mislead and damage not only adversaries, but also friendly interests or even the originator.

On the spectrum of economic intelligence-gathering, beyond overt competitive intelligence and the shadowy practice of disinformation, lies economic espionage. Favored methods on the clandestine side involve bribery of corrupt employees, "black-bag jobs" [burglary], eavesdropping and electronic bugging, and even stealing corporate trash. [Dudney:1995][30] Some

---

[29] U.S. Defense Department concerns that foreign interests are able to obtain critical U.S. technical data through the same methods are noted above, p. 7. See also Waller(1992).

[30] Foreign businesspersons in France, Japan, Korea, Argentina and Israel reportedly can expect anything left in hotel rooms to be "inspected," as well as routine bugging of phones, computers, and telefax machines. [Waller:1992; Ewell:1992; Gertz:1992a] Air France has been accused of plan-

East Asian nations are reportedly specialists at establishing and maintaining "false flag" operations—companies falsely claiming to be from third countries, but actually covert vehicles for commercial spying. [Ewell:1992; Gertz:1992a; Schweizer:1993:186ff][31]

The other "great game" of technology acquisition which often involves covert methods is practiced by the so-called "technobandits" [Melvern, et al:1984], expert commercial traders who obtain high-tech equipment on the open market, then illegally export it to prohibited end-users by circumventing trade embargoes and restrictions of the country of origin.[32] The equipment is "reverse-engineered" by the recipient nation [or company] in order to shortcut research and development time and cost.[33]

----

ting intelligence agents as passengers and flight attendants, and of bugging passenger conversation. [Reibstein, et. al:1991] Given the heavy involvement of many governments in economic espionage, it is also likely, if not certain, that signals intelligence ["SIGNT"] intercepts of international microwave communications by land, sea, air, and satellite spy systems are routinely obtained and used. NSA officials—who should know—are on record as warning that international corporate communications used by American companies are particularly vulnerable. [Gertz:1992a]

[31] This type of operation—not necessarily Korean—is often found in the chain of deception and diversion associated with the avoidance of export controls; see pp. 15ff, below.

[32] During the Cold War, the U.S. and most of its Western allies maintained an elaborate system of unilateral and multilateral statutory and administrative export controls designed to keep critical strategic technology away from the USSR and its allies. Some, but not all of these restrictions have been relaxed with cessation of open East-West hostility, but other controls remain as to the export of the U.S. defense technology [such as stealth aircraft], and materials or processes which could further the development of weapons of mass destruction by outlaw nations such as Iraq or Libya.

[33] Spying usually involves the illegal acquisition of information, product, or process. Techno-banditry, on the other hand, involves a legal source,

Obtaining the means of production is often more valuable than acquiring the actual product, and is a more often than not the objective of technological piracy. In a 1960 controversy over an export license for the sale of specialized ball-bearing grinding machines to the USSR, Secretary of Commerce Luther Hodges, opposing the license, articulated the logic of that notion, in a manner that is particularly relevant to the highly-competitive global economy of the 1990's:

> It is necessary to distinguish between giving away secrets, know-how, and capability. Our manufacture of these [miniature ball-bearings] is no secret—even the manner is not difficult to determine—but the capability to do it well and economically has taken years to develop and should not be sold to a potential adversary. . . . The situation is not one of selling our adversary a better 'club'—but machines which help to produce better 'clubs', faster and cheaper.[34]

Techno-bandits use the cover and trappings of legitimate business operations to obtain and export banned goods to prohibited end-users through "cut-outs"—other countries who for one reason or another fail or refuse to detect or enforce the export controls of the country of origin. False-labelling, false export declarations, dummy offices, bribery of customs officials

---

but an illegal disposition. Melvern, et al (1984:169) quote Anatoli Maluta, the leader of a Soviet-directed Silicon Valley ring of techno-bandits caught by the FBI, on the comparative risks of both methods: "there is no need for spies. You can get all this stuff [restricted semiconductor and integrated circuit technology] without any intrigue."

While civil and criminal penalties have been tightened by recent U.S legislation, getting caught is still viewed by the bandits as a simple business risk. The publicity attendant to an enforcement action may even serve to boost business as a "kind of advertisement." [Melvern, et al:1984;231]

[34] Melvern, et al (1984:262).

and personnel employed by common carriers, even old-fashioned smuggling are all tools of the techno-bandit's trade. [Melvern, et al:1984:passim][35]

---

[35] The Soviets always viewed the U.S. and Western Cold War export controls from the perspective of ideology; that is, as a form of economic and political warfare against the socialist nations, which was supported by the "myth" that the East was technologically dependent on the West. [Melvern, et al:1984:263-265] Party officials were used to relying on the "second" Soviet economy and its unofficial tolkachi [fixers], or the "shadow" economy and its black marketeers, to backstop the chronically lame "official" economy. Techno-bandits were [and probably still are] simply considered the tolkachi of foreign trade. [Melvern, et al:1984:61-61]

   Under the former Soviet Union, the KGB and the GRU conducted economic espionage operations through the sixty-plus Foreign Trade Organizations ["FTOs"] which were ostensibly engaged in the legal acquisition of trade through diplomacy, trade treaties, and open commercial arrangements. In actuality, FTO embassy personnel, consulates, and trade shows were "cover" for illegal espionage. The GRU operated under the aegis of the Soviet Defense Ministry, and the KGB functioned relatively autonomously [it was itself a Ministry] under the general authority of the Council of Ministers and the Politburo. The economic espionage operations of both were generally tasked by yet another Ministry, the Military-Industrial Commission ["VPK"], which was the coordinator of the Soviet "military-industrial complex" and the chief "consumer" of technology. [Melvern, et al:59ff]

   Much of this organizational arrangement did not survive the death of the Union, but the basic methodology is unchanged. The KGB and the GRU still conduct economic espionage operations under diplomatic cover as well as through "trade" organizations. [Ignatius:1992] See also "A Resurgence of Spy Fever Recalls Soviet Period," *Washington Times Weekly Edition*, September 3-10, 1995.

Countering Economic Espionage

Even in the absence of hard data, no one disagrees that the impact of economic espionage on the U.S economy and the U.S. national security interests is serious, and probably getting worse. No one disagrees that the open, liberal U.S. social and political order, as well as the nature of the world economy complicates the problem. Everyone disagrees about the cure.

Physical security—employee screening and supervision, guards, and electronic countermeasures—is effective but expensive and beyond the means of smaller businesses.[36] Further, product and process technology can't be fenced and guarded like military hardware, or locked up, to be occasionally looked at and admired like the Crown Jewels. Technology is useful only when used, that is widely dispersed in the stream of international commerce and thus vulnerable to unfair use or outright theft.[37]

---

[36] The Northrop Corporation estimates the industrial security costs associated with B-2 Stealth Bomber development and production since the late 1970s at "about $100 million per airplane." [NSI:1992d]

[37] Reich, Clancy and Seitz, Peter Rodman, and others, argue that because of this circumstance, modern technology cannot be "fenced" from copycats or thieves and, other than protecting purely military applications, the U.S. should probably not waste time or energy trying. Rather, these critics argue, private and governmental efforts should be devoted to achieving optimum industrial use of technology, rather than merely holding on to it. Further, Reich observes that technology development is increasingly exponential, not linear, and that a nation [or company] which doesn't concentrate on constructing a flexible industrial base to exploit state-of-the-art technology may have the knowledge but not the art, and will likely fall behind in competitiveness. [Reich:1987; Clancy and Seitz:1992; Ignatius:1992] Secretary Hodges made basically the same point in his 1960 testimony [see p. 14, above] but concluded that this was a reason for strict protective measures.

Private business interests in the U.S. have engaged in extensive consciousness-raising which has resulted in the adoption of
tighter security measures. [NSI:1992d; Yates:1993] The U.S.
Intelligence community has also been mobilized to deal with
the problem. The FBI has recognized economic espionage as the
"top national security threat posed by foreign intelligence oper-
atives," and has brought the Department of Defense and
Commerce Department technology experts into its reorganized
and upgraded counterintelligence program. [Seib:1992b;
Murray:1992]

The CIA had also entered the fray well before President
Clinton's July 1995 policy directive to the USIC. In 1992, former
Director Robert Gates announced that the CIA had increased its
emphasis on economic intelligence throughout the agency—
from analysis to covert action and wherever else required.
Foreign operations were to concentrate on other governments'
compliance with international trade agreements, and on efforts
those governments make to subvert U.S. businesses, technologies, and investments.[38] Particular priority will be given to
counterintelligence methods designed to detect commercial
"moles," and to counter bugging and other covert surveillance
of the U.S. business-persons abroad by foreign intelligence
agencies. [Gates:1992; Sinal:1992; Seib:1992][39] In May 1993, the

---

[38] That policy also reportedly includes exposure of cases of fraud and
bribery by which foreign corporations obtain an illegal "edge" over U.S. corporations bidding on foreign projects and purchases. [Keatley:1994;
Lippman:1994]

[39] Presumable, although it has not and would not be publicly
announced, U.S. electronic eavesdropping, or signals intelligence
("SIGINT") assets will also be utilized in support of CIA economic intelligence operations. Director Gates has also placed the development of human
intelligence assets ["HUMINT"]—live spies—high on the CIA agenda after

CIA provided a graphic demonstration of its new policy when it warned American aerospace companies scheduled to exhibit technology at the Paris Air Show, that the DGSE had targeted them for espionage at the show. [Smith:1993]

The CIA has been under constant pressure from Congress and some segments of the U.S. export business community to "fight fire with fire," that is to get involved in the same kind of economic espionage activities which other countries use against American industry. Former Director Gates resisted those pressures and repeatedly stated that the CIA ". . . . will not do commercial spying. Period." [Gates:1992; Seib:1992] His reasons were that those kinds of operations cause diplomatic problems in other countries, risk exposure of sources and methods, and present impossible choices to the CIA in terms of which private companies would be "favored" with such valuable information.[40]

---

years of primary reliance on technical means of intelligence-gathering—satellites, military platforms, etc. [Gates:1992] HUMINT is particularly effective for economic intelligence, satellites are not. The premier U.S. SIGINT operation, the National Security Agency ("NSA") certainly has this capability and is frequently accused by foreign government of facilitation the U.S. economic espionage. See "Using a Spyglass to Keep Track of America's Economic Interests," The Washington Post, June 27, 1990.

[40] Ewell (1992) quotes U.S. intelligence managers as asking: ". . . in an age of multinational corporations and global interactions, what defines an American company anyway?" Randall Fort's excellent [1993] monograph details all the contradictions and ambiguities which would be brought into play should the U.S. undertake a program of economic espionage. Warner [1993] has argued that such a program would patently violate numerous existing laws and treaties. In spite of these kinds of problems, Porteous [1993, 1994b] argues that even though "offensive" economic espionage is problematical, it should be a part of New World Order economic statecraft even as traditional espionage was [and likely still is] a part of diplomatic/military statecraft.

Gates' successor as CIA Director, James Woolsey, essentially continued Gates' basic approach while holding open the option of more aggressive action. Significantly, neither Woolsey, nor his successor, John Deutch, have explicitly ruled out a policy of economic espionage. [Omestad:1993][41]

If the CIA is to assume the principal institutional burden under the new 1995 directive (as well as undertake other covert operations in the economic area), questions relating to that Agency's competence and capability need to be examined. There are, for instance, significant indicators, from the Ames spy case, and elsewhere, that the CIA has yet to make a meaningful organizational transition from looking at the world through its 40-year Cold-War strategic lens, to an understanding of the economic determinants which drive the post-Cold War world.[42]

Former Director Gates' reference to possible diplomatic repercussions of American spying is interesting in view of the apparent absence of any diplomatic consequences of foreign spying on the U.S. relations with nations who routinely do it, including some of "our best friends."[43] The new Clinton direc-

---

[41] In a very farsighted manner which anticipated President Clinton's July 1995 directive, Cogan [1993:35] argued that CIA involvement in economic espionage to supplement government collection of open source information would be an inevitable consequence of increased emphasis on economic intelligence generally.

[42] See Walcott and Duffy:1994. See also "Our Stupid but Permanent CIA" (Senator Daniel Patrick Moynihan), *The Washington Post*, July 24, 1994, p. C3., and "Downspying the CIA," *The Washington Post*, March 5, 1995, p. C1.

[43] There appears to be no serious push either for diplomatic "linkage" ["quit doing it or suffer the consequences in another policy area"] or State Department demands for compliance with treaties and agreements such as international patent and copyright conventions, which economic espionage activities arguably violate.

tive, like the diplomatic agendas of other recent administrations, has omitted any reliance upon, or even a reference to, the diplomatic pressure point.

Finally, yet another area which is adversely impacted by economic espionage is the regime U.S. and multinational statutory and administrative export controls. These measures are increasingly directed to countering arms proliferation and, since the end of the Cold War, only partially fashioned to "protect" the U.S. economic interests in maintaining an endogenous technology base. Post-Cold War controls seem to be moving into at least two quite controversial dimensions. First, new programs such as the Enhanced Proliferation Control Regime, announced in 1990, place the burden on the American exporter to penetrate the covert mechanisms of the techno-bandits, a kind of expertise few businessmen possess or can afford; second, new legislation, such as the Exon-Florio Amendment to the 1988 Trade Bill, regulate foreign purchases of U.S. industries employing critical technologies which implicate "the national interest."

Export controls are both supported on the one hand as necessary to protect U.S. technology, and attacked on the other hand as burdensome, ineffective, and counterproductive to American industrial competitiveness. But, a collateral argument has not been substantially considered. If foreign economic intelligence-gathering, including covert espionage, is as pervasive and effective as it is claimed to be, legal restraints and regimes which seek to control technology outflow are simply unavailing as are the costs they impose on the U.S. economy.

Conclusion

This chapter has reviewed the issues and points, and some

of the primary authorities, which deal with the public and policy implications of foreign economic espionage targeted against U.S. technology. There is widespread agreement concerning the existence and extent of economic espionage, but little consensus as to its effect on the U.S. national interest or, assuming the effect to be harmful, how to counter it.

Three highly salient attributes of the post-Cold War "new world order" are likely causative factors in the worldwide increase of economic espionage, and are relevant to any consideration of policies designed to minimize or prevent its effects.

The first factor is the ascendance everywhere of economic issues over almost everything else that people used to think important.[44] The second is the understanding by most of the public—as well as policy elites—that there is no longer any practical or useful distinction between national economic relations and international economic relations. In other words, most national economies, like that of the U.S., are no longer islands where domestic preferences alone dictate outcomes. Third, "national security" is now seen more in terms of economic strength and vitality than in terms of purely military capability. The word "strategy" in the context of the Cold War evoked images of military alliance and power politics. Now it also encompasses national fiscal policy, commerce, trade, competitiveness, and—most importantly—the acquisition, adaptation, and application of cutting-edge technology.

Technology is not just the fuel which substantially powers

---

[44] Modern scholars such as Kenichi Ohmae [1995] argue that the global economic revolution is rapidly transforming and replacing the traditional nation-state with "natural economic zones" which aggregate people in terms of shared technological interests and economic activities, and not at all along familiar social and political lines.

a burgeoning world economy, it is increasingly the way that
politicians and economists keep score of both absolute and relative economic power which, in the global environment associated with the "new world order," increasingly equates to
national power. It is the level of technological sophistication
and capability which, among the nations, separates the industrialized and industrializing "haves" from the struggling
"have-nots." One may argue—and many do—about the injus-
tice, folly, or immorality of that phenomenon, but it is a fact of
life.

Further, technology needs to be understood as more than
inventions or abstract ideas-more even than product or process.
It is how technology is used which makes the difference and, as
noted and argued above, technology which is so protected that
it is actually or constructively withheld from the international
economy counts for nothing.

Finally, that attribute of modern technology which most
complicates counterespionage policymaking is what may be
called its "fungibility." This means simply that to a very significant degree, basic high-level technology may have interchange-
able applications within what we understand to be the commercial sector, and even between the commercial and military sectors. An example of a non-fungible technology with a purely
military application would be the warhead on a nuclear
missile.[45]

Guarding non-fungible warhead technology from foreign
spies is a fairly straightforward matter for counterintelligence
specialists. Dealing with fungible technology such as computers is ambiguous, difficult, and controversial as the 1993 fight

---

[45] The rocket itself is substantially fungible having as it does utility for
various commercial space programs.

over the sale of a Cray "supercomputer" to the PRC demon-strated. Was the computer to be used for weather prediction as PRC officials claimed? Or was it for their nuclear program as the U.S. defense and intelligence officials warned?

Both the hypothetical and the observed linkages between economics and technology and intelligence are as apparent as they are robust. Why then is policy formulation based on tradi-tional theoretical and empirical methodology so difficult, con-troversial, and problematic?

First, while all the elements of the posited linkages are well-understood within U.S. government policymaking cir-cles (including the Congress), the connective mechanics apparently are not. The same is also generally true of public perceptions. "Economics" as a national security concern for the general public and—apparently—for the usual array of foreign policy elites, either from the standpoint of threat or of opportunity, is still associated with the eye-glazing "dismal science" of old. The strategic economic challenge has pro-duced no analogue to George Kennan's famous 1947 "X" arti-cle which sounded the clarion call to recognize and resist Soviet expansionism, and helped to kick off American com-mitment to the Cold War.

Yet another significant part of the problem is the informa-tion base—or rather, more accurately, the lack of an authorita-tive information base. While there are some excellent industry-funded surveys showing dramatic increases in foreign intelli-gence activities which target U.S. economic interests, most of what is known is anecdotal. Industry surveys incorporate the best information available, but they are subject to challenge, generally because of measurement errors and inappropriate methodology. Ironically, these lacunae result in conditions which probably cause observers and analysts to understate the real extent of what is going on.[46]

At the point of policy formulation—especially legislation, where economic intelligence issues are concerned, most of the politicians don't "get it," or don't appear to "get it" because the electoral payoff is murky and—like the NAFTA issue-the short-term impact seems chancy and likely to be expensive.[47]

Journalists like Ron Yates, Jay Tuck, and Peter Schweizer are clearly doing the best job of analyzing and writing about economic intelligence issues, including espionage and counterespionage policy. The social sciences have lagged far behind because it is a mew and poorly-defined area, because it is a messy and normative topic characterized more by political rhetoric than scholarly discourse, and because whatever orderly analysis which does occasionally emerge is not at all theory-driven. Hopefully, academic attention and attendant analytical discipline will come as more comprehensive and more reliable data becomes available.

Based on all current indicators, this chapter concludes, first, that economic espionage targeted against U.S. industrial technology is at a very high level and is likely to increase; second, that the open, market-oriented global economy, essentially free of bipolar military competition, tends to facilitate economic espionage; and, third, that reliance on more intensive public

---

[46] Other complicating factors in gathering reliable and relevant data in this area include the necessary confidentiality of government agency records, and the reluctance of companies who have been victimized to risk public or shareholder repercussions as to the adequacy of management's defensive measures.

[47] See, e.g., Senate Select Intelligence Committee, August 5, 1993. At this particular hearing, industry representatives tried hard to articulate broad national policy issues such as expanded and better-coordinated counterintelligence resources. Senate Committee members consistently "talked past" these issues and fastened on parochial constituent preferences.

and private defensive measures based on current models will prove to be only a marginally effective if not altogether unsatis-factory cure.

References

Beardsley, Tim. 1985. "Technology Poaching: U.S. Haunts for Soviet Spies." *Nature*. v317 n_ p. 278. 9-26-85.

Berkowitz, Bruce D. and Allan E. Goodman. 1989. *Strategic Intelligence for American National Security* (Princeton Univ. Press: Princeton NJ).

Boren, David L. 1992. "The Intelligence Community: How Crucial?" *Foreign Affairs*. v71 n3. pp. 50-62 (Summer 1992).

Bush, Kieth. 1992. "An Overview of the Russian Economy." *RFE/RL Research Report*. v1 n25. pp. 49-54. June 19, 1992.

Carver, George A., Jr. 1990. "Intelligence in the Age of Glasnost." *Foreign Affairs*. v69 n3. pp. 148-166 (Summer 1990).

Chuah-Eoan, David. 1990. "New Trench Coats?" *Time Magazine*. v135 n_. pp. 40-42. 4-23-90.

Clancy, Tom and Russell Seitz. 1992. "Five Minutes Past Midnight and Welcome to the Age of Proliferation." *The National Interest*. n26. pp. 3-12 (Winter 1991/92); Comment and Reclama: Kenneth Adelman, and others. *The National Interest*. v27. pp. 106-112 (Spring 1992).

Clark, Evert, and Dave Griffiths. 1986. "Can a Democracy Afford the Free Flow of Disinformation?" *Business Week*. 4-14-86. p.43

Cogan, Charles G. 1993. "The New American Intelligence: An Epiphany." Working Paper #3, Project on the Changing Security Environment and American National Interests, John M. Olin Institute for Strategic Studies, Harvard University (January 1993).

Ewell, Miranda. 1992. "Who Snoops There: Friend or Foe?" *San Jose Mercury News*. 6-14-92. pp. 9-19.

Dudney, Robert S. 1985. "How Soviets Steal U.S. High-Tech Secrets." *U.S. News & World Report*. v99 n_. pp. 33-39. 8-12-85.

Eftimiades, Nicholas. 1994. *Chinese Intelligence Operations* (U.S. Naval Institute Press: Annapolis MD).

Fort, Randall M. 1993. "Economic Espionage: Problems and Prospects." Working Group on Intelligence Reform Papers, Consortium for the Study of Intelligence, Washington DC.

Foye, Stephen and Douglas L. Clarke. 1992a. "Military and Security Notes." *RFE/RL Research Report*, v1 n20. p. 27. May 15, 1992.

Foye, Stephen and Douglas L. Clarke. 1992b. "Military and Security Notes." *RFE/RL Research Report*, v1 n21. p. 39. May 22, 1992.

Foye, Stephen and Douglas L. Clarke. 1992c. "Military and Security Notes." *RFE/RL Research Report*, v1 n25. p. 70. June 19, 1992.

Gates, Robert. 1992. Interview. *Time Magazine*. v_ n_. pp. 61-62. 4-20-92.

Gertz, bill. 1992a. "The New Spy: '90s Espionage Turns Economic." *The Washington Times*. 2-9-92. p.A1.

Gertz, Bill. 1992b. "Japanese Intelligence Network Is All Business." *The Washington Times*. 2-9-92, P.A3.

Gertz, Bill. 1992c. "Friends, Foes Said To Employ Business Spies." *The Washington Times*. 4-30-92. p.A3.

Hanson, Philip. 1987. "Soviet Industrial Espionage." *The Bulletin of the Atomic Scientists*. v43 n_. pp. 25-29, April 1987.

Hanson, Philip. 1992. "The Russian Economy in the Spring of 1992." *RFE/Rl Research Report*. v1 n22. pp. 24-29. May 22, 1992.

Hedley, John Hollister. 1995. *Checklist for the Future of Intelligence*. Institute for the Study of Diplomacy (Georgetown Univ: Washington DC).

Holzer, Robert and George Leopold. 1992. "Pentagon Analysis to Stress Economic Threats." *Defense News*. 7-27/8-2-92. p. 4, 20.

Ignatius, David. 1992. "After the Wars: The Lonely Superpower." *The Washington Post*. 6-29-92. p.C1.

Kalugin, Oleg. 1992. Interview. ITAR-TASS. March 18, 1992. *Foreign Broadcast Information Service*. FBIS-SOV-92-053. March 18, 1992. pp. 38-39.

Kapstein, Jonathan, and Boyd France. 1985. "The West's Crackdown on High-Tech Smuggling Starts to Pay Off." *Business Week*. 7-29-85. pp. 46-48.

Keatley, Robert. 1994. "CIA Finds a New Focus: Espionage and Bribery That Hurt U.S. Business." *The Wall Street Journal*. 1-14-94. p.A8.

Knecht, G. Bruce. 1992. "Russia: Low on Fuel." *The Atlantic*, v270 n2. pp. 30-34 [August 1992].

Lee, Moon. 1993. "The Rise of the Company Spy." *The Christian Science Monitor*. 7-12-93. p. 7.

Lippman, Thomas W. 1993. "U.S. Seeks to Halt Illegal Payoffs by Foreign Corporations." *The Washington Post*. 12-3-93. p.A10.

Kuzichkin, Valdimir. 1990. *My Life in Soviet Espionage: Inside the KGB*. New York: Ivy Books.

Markoff, John. 1992. "A Public Battle Over Secret Codes." *The New York Times*. 5-7-92. p.D1.

Melvern, Linda, Nick Anning, and David Hebditch. 1984. *Techno-Bandits*. Boston:Houghton Mifflin.

Melville, Frank. 1985. "A Defector Warns: 'What Fools' " [Report of interview with unnamed former GRU Officer]. *Time Magazine*. v125 n_. p. 70. 5-27-85.

"Mikoyan Testing Advanced Version of MIG-29 Fighter." *Aviation Week & Space Technology*. v136 n25. p_. 6-22-92.

Munroe, Tony. 1992. "No-risk Bonds." *The Washington Times*. 4-15-92, p.C1.

Moon, Howard. 1989. *Soviet SST: The Techno-Politics of the Tupolev-144*. New York: Orion Books.

Murray, Frank J. 1992. "High-Tech Tracking Team Gets Off to Quiet, Slow Start." *The Washington Times*. 6-29-92. p.A3.

National Security Institute ["NSI"]. 1992a. "Globalization, Terrorism Pose New Threat to Information Security." *NSI Advisory*. v7 n6. pp. 6-7. January 1992.

National Security Institute ["NSI"]. 1992b. "Senate Intelligence Panel Chairman Sees Economic Spy Threat Growing." *NSI Advisory*. v7 n9. pp. 2-3. January 1992.

National Security Institute ["NSI"]. 1992c. "U.S. Business Secrets at

Risk in Global Economy, Study Finds." *NSI Advisory.* v7 n9. pp. 6-7. April 1992.

National Security Institute ["NSI"]. 1992d. "NISP, Economic Espionage Pose New Challenges to DoD Security." *NSI Advisory.* v7 n10. pp. 6-7. May 1992.

Newport, John Paul, Jr. 1985. "The Kremlin's High-Tech Hit List of U.S. Companies." *Fortune Magazine.* v112 n_. p. 120.11-25-85.

Ohmae, Kenichi. 1995. *The End of the Nation State* (Free Press: New York).

Omestad, Thomas. 1993. "Cloak and Dagger as R&D." *The Washington Post.* 6-27-93, p.C2.

Porteous, Samuel D. 1993. "Economic Espionage." in *Commentary*, No. 32. May 1993 (Canadian Security and Intelligence Service).

Porteous, Samuel D. 1994a. "Intelligence and Policy: What Is Constant? What is Changing?" in *Commentary*. No. 45. June 1994 (Canadian Security and Intelligence Service).

Porteous, Samuel D. 1994b. "Economic Espionage (II)." in *Commentary.* No. 46. July 1994 (Canadian Security and Intelligence Service).

Rahr, Alexander. 1991. "New Evidence of the KGB's Political Complixion Published." *RFE/RL Research Report.* v3 n3. pp. 1-5.

Rahr, Alexander. 1992. "The KGB Survives under Yeltsin's Wing." *RFE/RL Research Report.* v1 n13. pp. 1-4. March 27, 1992.

Reibstein, Larry, Christopher Dickey, and Douglas Waller. 1991. "Parles-Vous Espionage?" *Newsweek Magazine.* v118 n_. p. 40. 9-23-91.

Schweizer, Peter. 1993. Friendly Spies. *How America's Allies Are Using Economic Espionage To Steal Our Secrets.* New York: Atlantic Monthly Press.

Reich, Robert B. 1987. "The Rise of Techno-Nationalism." The *Atlantic Monthly.* v259 n5. pp. 62-69 (May 1987).

Seib, Gerald F. 1992a. "Spy vs. Spy: A Defector Describes a James Bond Life Inside the KGB." *The Wall Street Journal.* 2-12-92. p.A1, A3.

Seib, Gerald F. 1992b. "Business Secrets: Some Urge CIA to Go Further in Gathering Economic Intelligence." *The Wall Street Journal.* 8-4-92. p.A1, A7.

Senate Select Intelligence Committee. Transcript of Hearing 8-5-93, Federal Information Systems Corporation, Transcript #980420.

Sinai, Ruth. 1992. "Spy Agencies Will Shift Their Focus to Economics." *The Louisville Courier-Journal.* 4-14-92. p.A3.

Solobatin, Boris. 1992. Interview. ITAR-TASS. March 26, 1992, *Foreign Broadcast Information Service.* FBIS-SOV-92-060. March 27, 1992. p. 29.

Smith, Bruce A. 1993. "Espionage a Factor in Hughes Pullout." *Aviation Week & Space Technology.* 5-3-93. pp. 23-25.

Sussman, Vic. 1994. "Decoding the Electronic Future." *U.S. News & World Report.* 3-14-94. pp. 69-71.

"30% of Russian Spies Come in Out of the Cold." *The San Francisco Examiner.* 5-29-92. p.A9.

Tuck, Jay. 1986. *High-Tech Espionage: How the KGB Smuggles NATO's Secrets to Moscow.* New York:St. Martin's Press.

Walcott, John and Brian Duffy. 1994. "The CIA's Darkest Secrets." in *U.S. News & World Report.* Vol. 117, No. 1 (July 4, 1994).

Waller, Douglas. 1992. "The Open Barn Door." *Newsweek.* 5-4-92. p.58.

Waller, J. Michael. 1992. "Old Guard is Entrenched in New National Security Services." *American Security Council Foundation National Security Analysis.* 1-27-92.

Warner, William T. 1991. "The Crisis of State and Society in Gorbachev's Russia." unpublished paper. University of Kentucky. April 15, 1991.

Warner, William T. 1992a. "Vladimir Zhirinovsky: Traditional Nationalist, Reactionary Stalking Horse, or Modern Demagogue." unpublished paper. University of Kentucky. May 7, 1992.

Warner, William T. 1992b. "The Enhanced Proliferation Control Initiative." unpublished research paper. Center for Strategic & International Studies. Washington DC. July 21, 1992.

Warner, William T. 1993. "Economic Espionage: A Bad Idea." The *National Law Journal.* 4-14-93. pp. 12-13.

Warner, William T. 1994. "International Technology Transfer and Economic Espionage." in *International Journal of Intelligence and Counterintelligence.* Vol. 7 No. 2 (Summer 1994). pp. 143-160.

Yates, Ron. 1993. "Cold War: Part II." *The Chicago Tribune.* 8-29-93. p. 7-1, 6; 8-30-93, p. 2-1, 2.

Wright, Jeffrey W. 1991. "Intelligence and Economic Security." *International Journal of Intelligence and CounterIntelligence.* v5 n2. pp. 203-221 [Summer 1991].

Weber, Benjamin. 1994. "A Secret Warsaw Pact With the U.S. in the Cold War." *The Washington Post National Weekly Edition.* 2-21/27-94. pp. 18-19.

Zagorin, Adam. 1992. "Still Spying After All These Years." *Time Magazine.* v139 n6. pp. 58-59. 6-29-92.

Zaloga, Steven. 1992. "Ukraine, Russian Republic Quarrel Over Control of Military." *Armed Forces Journal International.* p. 15. January 1992.

Chapter 9

Economic Information Collection in Japan

Akio Kasai*

Introduction

With the end of the Cold War, it is said that intelligence agencies of the world superpowers are carrying out information collection targeted more at the economic field than at the traditional military field. Last February, five Americans, including the American embassy staff, were expelled from France for allegedly obtaining information on communications equipment and other information from officials at the French Prime Ministerial Office and the Ministry of Posts and Telecommunications. Recently, the U.S. government warned in the annual

---

* **Akio Kasai** is an advisor to Itochu Corporation. He served as a senior official at the Japanese Cabinet Intelligence and Research Office.

report to Congress that not a few nations were carrying out legal and illegal information collection targeted at U.S. industry and technology, threatening national security.

In spite of the world climate, Japan's intelligence agencies seem to remain almost unchanged in their activities. One reason may be that the agencies are small in scale; however, the most important reason would be that the strong influence of the Cold War still lingers on in East Asia. The changing international situation after the Cold War has led to the re-examination and re-evaluation of Japan's intelligence agencies in terms of their role and structure. These arguments, however do not cover the activities related with economic information collection.

Following is a summary of the history and characteristics of Japan's economic information collection, mainly in the private sector.

Choice to Survive on the Basis of Economy and Technology

This year marks the 50th anniversary of the end of World War II, after which Japan renounced war forever. Determined to recover from devastation, Japan set up a national policy to survive on the basis of economy. Soon enough, the Japanese economy recovered to pre-war production standards through a disproportionate production system that concentrated capital on key industries. Further development required updating obsolete facilities and improving technological standards, which were behind date.

The companies were determined to survive, making every effort to acquire patents to introduce the most advanced facili-

ties and technology from the U.S. and the industrialized countries in Europe. The Japanese government supported them until
its foreign currency savings were empty. Soon enough, the
Japanese companies became capable of competing on the international stage and paved the way to rapid economic development, using increasing exports as stimulus.

One of the elements essential to Japanese economic growth
may have been the appropriate government industrial policy,
named "Japan Inc." More essential elements, however, were the
ambition of the companies' management, the high standard of
national education, and the high standard of technology.

In particular, when introducing technology from other
countries, the companies and business organizations established wide surveillance networks to cover the U.S. and the
European industrialized nations and sent inspection missions
to pursue the most advanced and highest technology standard. Once the technology and facilities were brought back to
Japan, they were developed into higher, more innovative
uses.

Consequently, Japanese companies became well known for
their enthusiasm to introduce technology from other countries;
however, it also came to be known that Japanese science and
technology lacked originality and were good only at application
technology. It is fair to note, however, that the Japanese were
highly regarded for their originality in product development in
the earlier stages. Upon reaching the standard of the industrialized nations, the companies made great efforts in research and
development; this led to the high technology and high communications technology seen today.

As Japan reached the advanced industrial standards of the
U.S. and Europe and the era of technological competition
began, economic, trade, and industrial frictions surfaced

between Japan and these countries. That a country's economic prosperity is dependent on high industrial standards, science, and technology adds fuel to technological development competition.

Technological Innovation and Economic Conflicts

Under these circumstances, scandals related to technological plagiarism or breaches of COCOM (Coordinating Committee for Export Control) by Japanese companies began to be made known. The degrees of reactions from both inside and outside Japan suggested that the links between the economic, trade, political, and security issues were getting stronger.

Technological Plagiarism Incident

In June, 1982, in Silicon Valley, the most important site of U.S. advanced industry, six were arrested for industrial espionage by undercover agents of the FBI. The six, which included employees of a subsidiary company of Hitachi, Ltd. and Mitsubishi Electric Corporation, had tried to obtain information on IBM computers.

Hitachi was a manufacturer of computer hardware compatible with IBM products, while Mitsubishi had plans to enter the supercomputer market. Both companies were very interested in the basic computer software used in a new IBM supercomputer that had been released in November 1981.

In Silicon Valley, competition is tough among companies to develop advanced technology. Brokers and self-styled consultants are secretly active in stealing advanced technology and company secrets. Hitachi bought materials related to IBM's new generation of computers, which a former IBM engineer had stolen, from such a self-styled consultant. That Hitachi had confidential IBM information was revealed in the course of negotiation with another consultant, who promptly informed IBM of the matter. IBM appointed a former FBI counter-espionage agent to lead the investigation in collaboration with the FBI. The team posed as a consultant to lure Hitachi in. After Hitachi had paid a lot for the confidential materials they wanted, FBI agents arrested the parties involved at the site of handing over the materials.

It is unknown whether this case was Hitachi's unlawful information collection activities in the tough high technology development competition, or an ordinary illegal consulting activity which Hitachi happened to be involved in. Anyway, this incident gave a severe shock to both companies which had been trying to catch up with IBM and came close it. This case stimulated Hitachi to develop their own techno-logy.

COCOM Violation Incident

COCOM was one of the symbols of the East-West conflict during the Cold War. COCOM's objectives were preventing the export of civilian technology and products to the East, known as dual-technology, which could be used for military purposes.

COCOM regulations had been leniently implemented until the Cold War came to the end, after which the U.S. and other countries urged stricter implementation to prevent technology leakage to the East.

In December, 1985, a former president of a company trading with the East sent a letter to the COCOM office. The letter revealed the export of high tech products in violation of

COCOM regulations in which he was involved. The COCOM office subsequently demanded the Japanese government investigate the matter, but the government denied any wrongdoing had been committed.

The U.S. in those days was very alert to the USSR's intensification of nuclear forces and cautious about technological leakage in violation of COCOM regulations. Thus, the U.S. intelligence agencies began its own investigation and asked Japan to confirm facts through diplomatic channels. The U.S. submitted an independent investigation report to COCOM in January, 1987, reporting that the Toshiba Machine Co., Ltd. had exported their high technology milling machines to the USSR by way of Norway. The machines were being used for the production of submarines with low screw noise, which posed a significant threat to the West. In response, Japan and Norway re-investigated the case and found evidence that Toshiba Machine Co., Ltd. and a Norwegian company, Kongsberg AS., had exported in violation of COCOM regulations.

Toshiba Machine Co., Ltd. and Kongsberg AS. were punished according to their respective country's laws. Both companies were banned from exporting to the U.S. for three years: Toshiba Corporation, the parent company of the Toshiba Machine Co., Ltd., was similarly banned.

In addition, Norway's investigation revealed that companies of Sweden, France, West Germany, Italy, and England were also involved which put the violation of COCOM regulations on a larger scale than imagined.

In its early stages, this case created a stir between Japan and the U.S. due to unbalanced trade concerns and overall increasing economic frictions. The Japanese government took rapid measures, such as greatly intensifying export control procedures, to prevent the recurrence of similar incidents.

Violation of Export Regulations to Disputed Areas

As the Cold War came to the end, an increasing number of regional disputes arose from ethnic confrontation. It is necessary to control the export of weapons and other related materials to countries involved in disputes to avoid their intensification and military confrontation.

In July, 1991, the police charged the Japan Aviation Electronics Industry, Ltd. of illegal exporting air-to-air-missile parts to Iran.

Investigation began in response to information gathered from the U.S., who was investigating the Iran-Contra Affair. The company's overseas branch had asked for repairs of the U.S.-made air-to-air missile (Sidewinders) parts after which they were exported to Singapore and then Iran. The company submitted false documents to obtain permission to export the parts. This was the first prosecution case dealing with arms exports to a country fighting a war.

COCOM was dismantled with the end of the Cold War. A new international cooperation is now required to prevent the expansion of regional disputes in the Third World, the proliferation of biological or chemical weapons, and for other purposes.

Economic Information Collection in Japan

Submerged Activities

In contrast with the active economic information collection and the technology development competition by Japanese companies outside Japan, these activities are seldom made public in

Japan.

One reason for this may be that technological development in Japan, mainly for civilian usage, is comparatively open. Another reason may be that engineers and researchers are loyal to their companies, and they do not reveal much. However, the most likely reason is that companies do not dare rise the cases to the surface, concerned about their effects.

It was once said that the USSR had obtained 61.5% of its technological information from the U.S., 10.5% from West Germany, and 3% from Japan (as of 1980). In general, a small number of cases concerning activities of the foreign intelligence agencies become public in Japan. In May, 1992, a foreign government's trade and industrial officer to Japan bribed an executive of a trading firm of electronic parts. The officer demanded high performance semiconductor memory and transmission amplifier for communications satellites, in contravention of COCOM regulations. The executive ordered them falsely from a manufacturer and was arrested upon giving the products to the officer. The officer fled the country, ignoring an order to report to the prosecutor's office. This case was the first of its kind in five years.

Low Involvement of Economic Information Collection

During the Cold War, Japan's geopolitical location between the East and West made it an active site of intelligence operations of both sides. This led to the early formation of an counterespionage agency where supervision and discipline were conducted. In the earlier stages of the Cold War, Eastern intelligence agencies targeted Japanese political or military information. As the bipolar world order was fixed and the Japanese economy became competent, their interests shifted to economic and technological information. Most of the economic information collection incidents prosecuted in Japan involve foreign intelligence agencies.

A general information collection agency was finally established when Japan became independent in accordance with the talks with the Allied Nations. This agency has evolved into the Cabinet Intelligence Research Office. During the Cold War, the Cabinet Intelligence Research Office was known for its adequate analyses of international situations, particularly the political and military situations of East Asian communist countries. With the end of the Cold War, the Office now functions as a leading intelligence agency in Japan, coping with complicated international situations using its wide range of sources and analysis capabilities. It can not be denied, however, that the Office remains too small in scale to be capable of dealing with current circumstances of increasing complication and liquidity. It is hoped that the Office will be developed into an agency suitable to Japan's national power and responsibilities as expected on the international stage.

Roles of Intelligence Agencies in the Future

The era of political and military confrontation between the East and West has ended, as has the threat of large-scale war. Yet there has been a rise in economic and technological confrontations, even between traditionally friendly countries. Such confrontations are still complex and not transparent; needless to say, a country's security cannot be discussed only from an economic point of view.

Small in scale but large in number, regional disputes are arising all over the world, stemming from ethnic, religious, and regional struggles. They are destabilizing elements, and their outcomes cast a great influence over world peace. Non-proliferation of nuclear, biological, and chemical weapons, terrorism, global drug trade, criminal organizations, environmental problems-these are the new tasks which all nations must cope with together. In tackling some of these global problems, it is appropriate to look to the intelligence agencies and their accumulated experiences, human and material resources, and know-how, in addition to administrational and supervisional measures.

As competition over the development of various kinds of high technology gets tougher, the number of cases involving illegal acquisition of industrial secrets or technological information is sure to rise. This would lead to political tension between the countries concerned; therefore they should be avoided properly. It is important that companies engage in fair and reserved competition, and that they take steps to prevent the leakage of confidential information. The administration must exercise strict supervision and discipline; the police must exercise more strict control.

It is disputable how and to what extent the intelligence agencies are entitled to intervene in such economic fields. It is rational that a specific piece of economic information draw security-related concerns; economic friction usually develops into political confrontation. We also cannot draw a line between civilian and military high technology, which means they are equal. The more individual and the more specific a theme is, the more an individual company's interests are threatened. Even in this era of economic competition, the existence of a country is not dependent only on economic information. The increase of multinational enterprises and internationalization of capital have brought companies' interests over borders, which has caused conflicts with a country's national interests or national security. It is a delicate question: how far can intelligence agencies be involved in or interfere with competition between companies to defend the country and protect national interest? In particular, indiscreet operations by intelligence agencies to otherwise friendly countries could harm cooperative relations which are required for the resolution of global problems. This is why intelligence agencies are required to be very discreet and careful in how far involved they are in economic information collection.

Japan, a country of advanced technology, has benefited from an orderly and fair international economy. With its policy of economic and technological national growth. Japan must now take proper measures to protect this environment through a joint effort of the government and the people.

Chapter 10

Trade Secrets, UR Efforts, and Korea's Position

Jang-Hee Yoo*

Introduction

In modern industrial society, development of technologies and firm specific strategies are essential to a firm's production and sales activities. All firms invest substantial amounts of capital and labor in the development of new technology and sales strategies in order to obtain a competitive advantage in the market.

The term 'trade secrets' (also 'proprietary information' or 'undisclosed information') refers to all information related to

---

* **Jang-Hee Yoo** is President of Korea Institute for International Economic Policy. He is a member of the Foreign Policy Advisory Committee, Segyehwa Promotion Committee, and the Korea-America 21st Century Council.

technology, techniques, strategies, sales plans, and so forth which are developed to give a firm a competitive edge in the market and are kept as secrets within the firm through considerable effort. Know-how is an example of a secret; so are lists of consumers, investment plans, and marketing strategies.

The trade secrets of a particular firm may provide valuable information to competing firms since they have independent economic value; thus, they may be subject to espionage. These firms should be able to protect their trade secrets in order to maintain their competitive advantage in the market.

The need for trade secrets may be discussed from several perspectives. First, trade secrets have come to play a more critical role in firms' activities, both qualitatively and quantitatively. Development of high technology and information have more important effects nowadays on a firm's activities. Competition among firms has become more severe than ever. In addition, consumers look for products which can satisfy their diverse tastes. As a result, a firm's performance is dependent upon firm-specific know-how in production and sales activities. Also, exchange of this kind of information between firms has become active in recent years. A side effect of these changes in market conditions has been an increase in the infringement upon proprietary information through unfair methods. This calls for the need to establish some protective measures for trade secrets.

In the grand scheme of things, the importance of trade secrets within a particular industry has increased substantially. As information becomes more important and technology becomes more complex in modern industrial society, development of new technological know-how has greater significance than ever before. In addition, unpatented technology and information are of greater importance.

Moreover, in the current market environment of harsh competition and diverse consumer demand, distinctive market strategies are essential to obtain a competitive advantage. Thus, trade secrets regarding not only technological know-how but also sales activities, such as consumer mailing lists, have come to play a very important role, particularly in service industries (distribution, fast food, and leisure industries).

One can also argue that trade secrets play an important role not only for individual firms and specific industries but also in forming a foundation for Korea's economic development and in sustaining industrial technological development and competitiveness. Therefore, regarding trade secrets, orderly market competition should be promoted. By doing so, technological innovation, development of new sales strategies, and subsequent improvement in product quality, and the lowering of price can be achieved through fair competition. Thus, protection of trade secrets can contribute to the improvement of social welfare.

Furthermore, in order to promote fair competition, unfair trade secret-acquiring activities must be regulated. Such undesirable activities reduce incentives for further research and development by other firms in the industry and have negative effects on fair competition.

There have been considerable efforts to protect trade secrets, both internationally and domestically. This paper will briefly review multilateral efforts made for the protection of trade secrets during the UR negotiation. Korea's position on the issue will be discussed in the latter part of the paper. The following section provides some definitions of terms often used in the discussion of proprietary information.

Definitions

Many shy away from dealing with matters concerning proprietary information in fear of the complexity of the issue. In truth, however, the issue is not as complex as it seems. The following is a glossary of definitions to help elucidate the jargon of proprietary information.[1]

Confidential

Items or information that are secret and for which access is limited to certain people within an organization. Company documents often are marked confidential to denote that they are proprietary. However, confidential information is not necessarily a trade secret. To be a trade secret, it also must have value to the company's competitors. A confidential customer list, for example, would not be protected if the company's clients were obvious to everyone else in the industry.

Copyright

An exclusive legal right to reproduce, publish and sell the matter and form of a literary, musical or artistic work. Some companies copyright instruction manuals and training videos.

---

[1] All definitions are quoted directly from Kathleen Murray, "HR Takes Steps To Protect Trade Secrets," *Personnel Journal*, June 1994, pp. 100.

Intellectual Property

Ideas, processes, slogans or other intangible property that are created at an organization and give it added value or an edge over competitors. In recent years, this area has stretched a great extent.

Non-compete Agreement

A written agreement in which an employee agrees not to compete with his or her employer by working for a competitor or becoming a competitor, usually for a specified period. These agreements often are tied to pay or severance packages.

Patent

A legal right or privilege that gives an inventor the exclusive right to make, use or sell an invention for a specified period of time. Patents can be obtained on products, but often on processes as well, such as a patented process to manufacture a new drug or a toaster.

Trade Secret

Any formulas, ideas, customer lists, documents or knowledge that are proprietary to an organization and generally not known in the industry. A company generally must make efforts to keep this information confidential and prove that the information gives it a competitive edge.

Trademark

A registered word or device (logo) that points to origin or ownership of merchandise to which it is applied and gives the owner the legal right to proceeds from making or selling it.

UR TRIPs and Trade Secrets

The issue of trade secrets was one of the most focal and controversial issues in the UR negotiation on Trade-Related Intellectual Property Rights (TRIPs).

Due to the covert nature of trade secrets, it is very hard to define in advance the range of protection and to write up legal rights for them. In addition, trade secrets cannot be disclosed to others, whereas other legal rights such as patents are required to be open to the public. For example, when a patent is granted on an invention, the inventor acquires exclusive rights for the patent for a certain period of time (15 years in Korea, 17 years in the U.S. and Japan, 20 years in Germany, and so forth), while at the same time, relevant information on the patented invention is disclosed to the public in order to encourage further research and development. The basic underlying principle of the patent system is to encourage research and development.

Therefore, due to the aforementioned difference between patents and trade secrets, all developing and some advanced countries have expressed strong opposition to the proposal to include protection of trade secrets in the UR negotiation. However, since Japan and northern European countries have switched their positions to favor protection, protection of trade secrets was included in the Agreement on Trade-Related

Aspects of Intellectual Property Rights, including Trade in Counterfeit Goods (UR TRIPs Agreement).

On the protection of trade secrets, the UR TRIPs Agreement, Article 39, Paragraph 1 states:

In the course of ensuring effective protection against unfair competition as provided in Article 10bis of the Paris Convention (1967), Members shall protect undisclosed information in accordance with paragraph 2 below and data submitted to governments or governmental agencies in accordance with paragraph 3 below.

The definitions for trade secrets and the right to protect them are included in the UR TRIPs Agreement, Article 39, Paragraph 2:

Natural and legal persons shall have the possibility of preventing information lawfully within their control from being disclosed to, acquired by, or used by others without their consent in a manner contrary to honest commercial practices so long as information:
- is secret in the sense that it is not, as a body or in the precise configuration and assembly of its components, generally known among or readily accessible to persons within the circles that normally deal with the kind of information in question (undisclosed information);
- has commercial value because it is secret (usefulness);
- has been subject to reasonable steps under the circumstances, by the person lawfully in control of the information, to keep it secret (condition on the management of secrecy).

Therefore, according to the UR TRIPs Agreement, trade secrets are protected to prevent unfair competition (Article 39, Paragraph 1). The Agreement also guarantees the holder of trade secrets the right to prohibit the disclosure of information acquired through dishonest commercial practices and the unauthorized acquisition and use of trade secrets by third parties (Article 39, Paragraph 2).

While other intellectual property rights, such as patents, are protected as 'legal rights,' negotiators agree that trade secrets should be protected in a manner to prevent and regulate unfair access of third parties to proprietary information, such as technological know-how and managerial secrets.

Korea's Legal and Institutional Arrangements

Instead of additional legislation on protective measures for trade secrets, Korea has been protecting trade secrets since December 1991 by revising its Unfair Competition Prohibition Law. This is consistent with the UR TRIPs agreement in which trade secrets are protected as a means to prohibit unfair competition, not as a legal right.

In Article 2, Clause 2 of the Unfair Competition Prohibition Law, a trade secret is defined as "technological or managerial information on production, sales, and other business activities which is not generally known in the industry; has independent economic value; and has been kept as a secret with considerable efforts." This definition is consistent with international standards since it includes both technological and managerial information. At the same time, the definition satisfies the following conditions for trade secrets as defined in the UR TRIPs agreement: (1) undisclosed information, (2) usefulness, and (3) condition on the management of secrecy.

Violations of the above law include the following activities: (1) acquisition, use, and disclosure of trade secrets through unfair methods such as stealing, deceiving, and threatening; (2) acquisition, use, and disclosure of trade secrets with prior knowledge of any involvement of unfair practices in the acquisition of relevant information or without any prior knowledge of involvement of unfair practices due to significant negligence; (3) disclosure of secrets by an employee; (4) use and disclosure of trade secrets by a person who is obligated by contract to keep the trade secret undisclosed (Article 2, Clause 3).

Regarding legal enforcement at executive levels against employees who unlawfully disclose and use trade secrets of a firm, the law requires the holder of a trade secret to file charges against the violator. (A personal accusation against the violator is required.) This is to promote harmony between the protection of trade secrets and the rights of the employee. The law intends to prevent criminal charge abuses and where possible, to let relevant cases be resolved as civil affairs.

Some Representative Cases

Recently, the domestic market has been experiencing drastic and rapid changes. As a result of on-going liberalization and informatization in the domestic market, competition has become much steeper than ever before. Consequently, disputes over the violation of trade secrets, not only between domestic firms but also between domestic and foreign firms, have increased substantially. Following are summaries of some representative cases of infringement upon trade secrets in the domestic market[2]:

---

[2] Chung, Gap-Young, "Protection of Trade Secret and Firms' Managerial

Case 1: Newly Developed Technology

Kyung-Shin Industry Inc. has developed new technology related to pattern embossment on synthetic leather with linked patterns almost identical to natural leather. This technology was not available, even in Japan to which Kyung-Shin Industry exported its synthetic leather.

An employee who worked as an errand boy during the development of the relevant technology recorded ways to imitate instruments and raw materials used in the synthetic leather development process. As he moved to another firm, he helped produce synthetic leather similar to that produced by Kyung-Shin and sold it to domestic luggage bag makers at a much cheaper price. These luggage bags were then exported to Japan. Later, the imitated synthetic leather itself was exported to Japan. Under these circumstances, the Japanese importer of Kyung-Shin's products expressed strong concern over the situation.

Consequently, Kyung-Shin filed a civil suit against the imitator of its technology for violating the Unfair Competition Prohibition Law and requested provisional banning of production, compensation for damages, and a written apology in a newspaper. However, the court hearing took too long to provide prompt assistance. Moreover, the person who stole the technology from Kyung-Shin moved around from one company to another and continued to produce the imitation product.

In the end, several defendant companies agreed not to produce and sell imitation products in the future. Instead of a writ-

Strategy," Institute of International Trade Management, February 1992, pp. 101-106.

ten apology in a newspaper, they agreed to distribute apology notes to luggage makers. Therefore, despite all of the damages done, Kyung-Shin did not receive any practical compensation.

Case 2: Process Technology

The following is a case in which a skilled worker of a Korean company, after learning the production process, sold critical process technology to a plastic manufacturer in Taiwan.

As the process technology was being developed in Korea, a Taiwanese plastic manufacturer invited the Korean worker to Taiwan for a tour. Eventually, with the help of the employee the Taiwanese firm learned the process technology without paying any significant development costs.

A prime example would be one in which a Southeast Asian worker, while employed in Korea, learns the process technology of Korean firms and then returns to his country with the critical knowledge.

Case 3: Distribution Know-How

Korea-Seven Inc. has been paying a considerable amount of royalty to Seven-Eleven of the U.S. for its consultation on distribution and management know-how.

In 1989, after an unpleasant argument with his superiors over his managerial incompetence, a deputy manager in the product development department of Korea-Seven stole copies of summaries on distribution networks, sales plans, and other confidential documents. Eventually, he sold these confidential documents to Korea-Seven's domestic competitor, Dong-Yang Mart. The deputy manager in question was caught and charged with dereliction of duty and larceny of the firm's properties.

Conclusion

Technology and information not only play a critical role in the development of industry but also have a crucial effect on firm management in the current world economic environment. Consequently, all industrialized countries are investing heavily in both basic sciences and in the development of industrial technologies in order to be competitive in the world market. In addition, various supportive and protective institutional measures are being implemented to promote technological innovation and development.

Individual firms are also putting tremendous efforts into research and development in order to improve the quality of their products and services and to be competitive in the market. From high-tech to service industries, competition among firms to obtain higher market shares through the development of technological and managerial know-how has become more intense than ever. This phenomenon is becoming more apparent as the informatization of the economy progresses and the share of the service industry in the world market expands.

In Korea, as the opening of the domestic market continues and the transfer of labor among industries increases due to industrial restructuring, technology and other proprietary information have become major issues to be dealt with. Recently, relocation of employees among domestic firms has increased significantly, as has contracting of licensing agreements between domestic firms. Consequently, the possibility of infringement upon trade secrets has risen in Korea.

Furthermore, as foreign firms start to make full-scale investments in the Korean market due to the progress of Korea's liberalization plan, the possibility for disputes between domestic and foreign firms over trade secrets could gradually increase. In particular, highly competitive industries where large-scale investments are essential and labor is scarce are more likely to have such disputes due to employee scouting, industrial espionage, fraudulent use and imitation of sales information, and so forth.

Therefore, in order to properly respond to the ongoing changes in the Korean market and to promote fair competition and active research and development, the following strategies ought to be carried out by the government and by firms. First, the importance of trade secrets must be recognized. Firms must make proper efforts to manage their trade secrets and keep them confidential with the full understanding of the legality and the scope of legal protection. Second, by strengthening the education and the monitoring of employees, firms will be able to prevent infringement upon trade secrets. Since the majority of trade secret violations are committed by employees who have access to information, reorganizing the secret management systems and educating employees will have a substantial effect on the prevention of unlawful outflow of proprietary information. Third, firms must be ready to properly respond to the liberalization and the opening of the Korean market. Korean firms could heighten their international credibility and actively promote transfer of technology from foreign firms by managing their trade secrets properly. Firms should be ready to compete fairly with foreign firms as well as with other domestic firms in a liberalized domestic market. Fourth, the Korean government should endeavor to minimize damages caused by the infringement upon trade secrets in the domestic market by actively publicizing and properly applying a trade secret protection system. Moreover, the government may play an active role by providing educational programs to firms, informing them of ways to better manage their trade secrets under the current institutional arrangement.

In sum, only with such active efforts by firms and the government will Korean firms be able to obtain and maintain their competitiveness in the global market.

References

Chung, Gap-Young. "Protection of Trade Secret and Firms' Managerial Strategy." Institute of International Trade Management, February 1992.

Murray, Kathleen. "HR Takes Steps to Protect Trade Secrets." *Personnel Journal*, June 1994.

Sohn, Chan-Hyun. "UR Negotiation on Trade Secrets and Its Effects." mimeo, Korea Institute for International Economic Policy, 1994.

"Final Act Embodying the Results of the Uruguay Round of Multilateral Trade Negotiations." Economic Planning Board, December 1993.

Chapter 11

Rethinking National Intelligence:
Comparative Implications[1]

Chung-in Moon*, with Judy E. Chung**

The international conference which the Korean Society for the Study of National Intelligence organized was significant on several accounts. Although panelists were drawn largely from practitioners rather than scholars, the quality of papers was excellent, and discussions were insightful and penetrating. The

---

* **Chung-in Moon** is Professor of Political Science at Yonsei University and Executive Secretary of the Korean Society for the Study of National Intelligence.

** **Judy E. Chung** is a graduate student at the Graduate School of International Relations, Yonsei University. She holds her B.A. from Columbia University and has worked as a student journalist.

[1] This chapter presents an analytical summary of ideas and opinions emerged during the conference. We would like to acknowledge contributions made by panelists whose papers are featured here and by those who served as chair and discussants of each panel. Their names and affiliations appear in appendix.

encounter between William Colby, former director of the Central Intelligence Agency, and Vadim Kirpitchenko, a leading figure of the Russian Foreign Intelligence Service and formerly KGB, was stimulating and rewarding. Though arch rivals during the Cold War, they not only showed unusual personal warmth and friendship but also enhanced the vitality of the conference through unfailing participation and discussion. Their amicable interactions and candid exchange of views were an eloquent testimonial to the passage of time from confrontation to cooperation.

The conference yielded other positive dividends to the study of national intelligence. Aviezer Yaari offered us fresh insights into the strengths and weakness of the Israeli national intelligence system with analytical wit, empirical depth, and rich policy implications. Although the Japanese national intelligence system has drawn intellectual and practical curiosity, very little is known about it. Akio Kasai's discussion of Japan's national intelligence, though limited, made up for the lacunae by offering a comprehensive overview. As with Japan, South Korea's national intelligence system has remained very much untouched. Most works, which are published in Korean, focus on political abuse and misuse of security apparatus, aiming at sensational readership, rather than on the objective assessment of intelligence community. In this regard, Chung-in Moon and his colleagues made a timely and significant contribution to the understanding of the national intelligence system in South Korea. While most chapters approached national intelligence from the producers' point of view, Bruce Weinrod suggested new directions for U.S. national intelligence reforms from the consumers' perspective.

Equally interesting were discourses on economic intelligence. William Warner's discussion presented a lucid and penentrating analysis of foreign countries' economic espionage works in the U.S. and American counter-economic espionage. Warner raised several important analytical and empirical issues concerning the concepts and operationalization of economic espionage. While Akio Kasai gave a general portrait of Japan's economic intelligence system, Jang-Hee Yoo renewed an emphasis on the importance of economic and industrial intelligence by elucidating South Korea's experiences in dealing with trade negotiations involving the Uruguay Round.

Discussions throughout the conference have touched several salient theoretical, empirical, and policy issues in the study of comparative national intelligence. They include: the issue of articulating changing national security priorities to the function and scope of national intelligence; operational modes of national intelligence system; the role of national intelligence organizations in ensuring national vs. regime security; directions for organizational reforms; debates on human intelligence vs. technical intelligence; myths and realities of economic intelligence; quality of political leadership and national intelligence community; and the significance of intelligence cooperation.[2] We will discuss each of these issues briefly as a way of setting up a new agenda for the study of comparative national intelligence.

National Security and National Intelligence

Panelists have all agreed that the concept of national securi-

---

[2] Working Group on Intelligence Reform of the National Consortium on the Study of Intelligence in the U.S. has published an interesting monograph series (10 volumes) dealing with some of these issues. Although emphasis is placed on the case of the U.S. they are very timely and illuminating.

ty should be subjected to new interpretations. National survival through military self-help is still important, but it cannot and should not overrule other security concerns.[3] In an age of waning massive nuclear threats and major interstate military conflicts, economic security involving growth, welfare, stability, and employment is as crucial as military security concerns. It is even more so because of an increasingly competitive international economic environment. Enhancing a competitive edge through technological innovation from within and the acquisition of cutting-edge technology from abroad has become a new slogan of national security for many countries.[4] Maintaining an optimal ecological carrying capacity to ensure the organic survival of a national population was also pointed out as a newly emerging security concern. Ecological security is predicated on securing a stable supply of food, energy, and resources as well as sustaining environmental integrity.[5] Finally, issues pertaining to societal stability, which have traditionally belonged to the domain of domestic public safety, are being increasingly recognized as a major national security agenda. Several public safety issues are characterized by the blurred demarcation between domestic and international boundaries. Penetration of international organized crime networks and the endangering of public safety, drug trafficking and the destruction of social fabric,

---

[3] See R. Ullman, "Redefining Security," *International Security,* Vol. 8 (Summer 1983); J. Mattews, "Redefining Security," *Foreign Affairs,* Vol. 68 (Spring 1989); Edward Azar and Chung-in Moon, *Third World National Security: Internal and External Management* (London: Edward Elgar Press, 1988).

[4] W. Sandholtz, M. Borrus, and J. Zysman et. al., *The Highest Stakes: The Economic Foundation of the Next Security System* (New York: Oxford University Press, 1992).

[5] See Dennis Pirages, *Global Techno-politics* (Pacific Grove, California: Brooks and Cole, 1989).

threats from international terrorist attacks, and transnational computer terrorism and information disorder all exemplify the national security dimensions of social issues. For some countries inflicted with protracted ethnic conflicts, maintaining communal harmony and social integration may well be considered the principal national security concern.

How should the role of national intelligence be redefined in light of changing priorities of national security? Most panelists agreed that the scope of national intelligence should be expanded to cover these newly emerging issues. Yet, it should not undercut conventional functions, such as the collection of political and military intelligence. Despite the rise of a new security environment where distinguishing friends from foes has become a difficult task, every nation is still concerned about its military security. Countries might want to monitor political and military moves of even friendly nations in order to reduce conflicts while enhancing cooperation. In this regard, defense intelligence targeting major actors' early warning, strategic moves, force structure and deployment, weapons development and acquisition, and proliferation of nuclear weapons and missile technology constitutes the core of national intelligence. Political intelligence on power structure, quality and intention of political leadership, and overall political trends are equally critical. As shall be discussed below, for all its purported importance, the role of economic intelligence is ambiguous and even redundant. Its targets are less clear, the distribution of its benefits could be troublesome, and the contribution of national intelligence services, as opposed to the private sector, is questionable. Most panelists, however, believed that despite overlapping jurisdictions among domestic agencies, national intelligence services should actively engage in societal security concerns such as organized crime, international terrorism, drug trafficking, and transnational computer terrorism. Interestingly, ecological security issues drew less attention. This can be attributed to a lack of immediacy, salience, and intensity in security discourses.

Despite the overwhelming consensus on the expanded role of national intelligence in the post-Cold War era, several caveats, mostly involving institutional barriers, were pointed out. First, it might not be easy to make a conceptual reorientation of intelligence services for non-military issues. The Cold War mindsets are still dominant, and removing such perceptual and institutional inertia is not simple. Second, venturing into new areas requires increased investment in human and financial resources along with major organizational reforms. Fiscal hardship and waning public support of national security issues, common to virtually all nations on the earth, are likely to impede such moves. Finally, the domain of non-military intelligence overlaps that of other domestic agencies. The extension of national intelligence functions into these areas is tantamount to trespassing bureaucratic turfs of other agencies, which can in turn intensify inter-agency conflicts, posing a major coordination dilemma. Thus, realigning missions of national intelligence along changing priorities of national security might be a challenging task in reality.[6]

Modus Operandi in National Intelligence:
Preconception or *Tábula Rása*

Another major issue concerns operational modes of national intelligence; whether intelligence organizations should have

---

[6] See B. Berkowitz and A. Goodman, "Why Spy and How in the 1990s?" *Orbis*, Vol. 36, No. 2 (Spring 1992); Ernest May, "Intelligence: Backing into the Future," *Foreign Affairs*, Vol. 73, No. 3 (Summer 1992).

their own preconceptions of national security and intelligence or not. General Yaari, for example, argued that intelligence organizations should have their own conceptual framework through which they collect and analyze information. In theory, political leaders define priorities of national security and national intelligence operations. In reality, however, they often fail to give a good sense of national security and to make adequate intelligence requirements not only because of electoral cycles and changes of leadership, but also because of a lack of expertise and information. If intelligence services are devoted solely to satisfying the needs and demands of their leaders, they could suffer from inconsistent and incoherent situations. A well refined preconception is thus required in order to produce an accurate and objective assessment of security reality. Collecting and delivering naked information to final consumers without due processing can deal a critical blow to national security. Suppose the Syrian army of 10-12 divisions is engaging in a major military maneuver for 'peacetime' preparedness. With its combat readiness and modern weapons system, it can be assumed that the Syrian army can attack Israel at any time. This being the case, Israel should put all of its military resources on the border with Syria, creating a security vacuum in other border areas. It is the task of the Israeli intelligence organization to judge the preemptive or offensive nature of the Syrian military maneuver with its own conceptual framework, so that it can inform political leaders in deploying and redeploying military forces. Transmission of naked information can alarm political leaders and people, triggering chaos and disorder in Israel.

Yaari's position was strongly challenged by General Kirpitchenko. Kirpitchenko counterargued that national intelligence organizations should be something like *tábula rása*. It should not possess its own preconceptions or agenda. If so, it can undermine the entire intelligence process. Intelligence organizations should get requirements from political leaders and deliver what they want as they are. Evaluation and judgment should be solely left to the leaders. Intelligence organizations cannot and should not be an active party in the actual making of national security policy. This belongs to the domain of policy-makers. Intelligence organizations should support and facilitate policy-makers by providing them with objective information on what they are concerned with. Should they cross that boundary, they become politicized, the intelligence they offer becomes biased, and national security itself can be endangered. When and if intelligence service is captured by false conceptions, its consequences can be grave. For example, the Russian intelligence service felt for years that all third world countries leaned toward socialism. This misconception significantly hindered Russian intelligence operations. Likewise, if Israel is obsessed with a preconception that Arabs are its constant enemy, then there would be no peace agreements between the two. Thus, intelligence services should avoid being captured by preconceptions or false images. They should be guided by political leaders.

Colby has suggested an alternative way focusing intelligence. In theory, an intelligence service goes to its customers, and asks them what they want to know, thereby it develops a set of requirements. Then, it defines these requirements, and sends them out to intelligence officers to collect and analyse information with respect to these requirements. That's theory. But what actually happens is that customers usually provide a list covering every last detail in fear of leaving something out. The intelligence service looks at the list, decides it is too long to be useful, throws it out, and collects the information it thinks customers ought to know. Thus, any good intelligence officer should be aware of the situation he faces, but he should be also attentive to what his clients need to know. In view of this, intelligence services should develop a short set of key intelligence questions, omitting those which are not important. Thus, prioritizing intelligence collection and analysis is essential. However, who decides what is important is the customer-the president, then the cabinet, and then the National Security Council in the United States. Weinrod also concurs with Colby's observation. The supply of raw data seems less useful to consumers. In reality, less than one percent of all data draws policy-makers' attention. An analysis of the situation and the presentation of contending views is much more appreciated. In this sense, there must be an adequate balancing of what customers need and of what intelligence services consider important.

Depoliticizing Intelligence Service: National vs. Regime Security

There was a broad consensus on the issue of depoliticizing intelligence services. National intelligence should be the instrument of national security, not regime security. Politicizing intelligence services for the cause of regime security not only undercuts national security, but also eventually undermines regime security *per se*. However, good performance by intelligence services and subsequent improvement of regime popularity is acceptable and even desirable. In reality, the boundary between direct political use of intelligence services and indirect or circumventive policy utilization is often blurred, resulting in political sensationalization and the deformity of intelligence services. Therefore, it is imperative to make a clear legal and insti-

tutional demarcation between the two. In doing so, profession-
alization of intelligence officers, political neutralization of intelligence services, and constant control and oversight over intelligence organizations are required. Such efforts are, however,
fundamentally constrained by the type of political regime.
Under democratic regimes, depoliticization of intelligence services can be easily ensured through legal and institutional
arrangements. But authoritarian regimes are much more prone
to use them for their survival and power consolidation. South
Korea under past authoritarian regimes, SAVAK in Iran under
Shah, and intelligence services in most developing countries
present classical examples of the politicization of security and
intelligence services.

Kirpitchenko suggested an interesting check list on this
matter in light of his Russian experiences. He delineated six
points crucial to the successful working of national intelligence
in a normal, democratic state. First, control and secrecy must be
the primary guiding principles for intelligence activities in
democratic states. Legislative control of intelligence activities
over budget, directions, and forms and methods should be
institutionalized. Yet, legislative control should not compromise
the secrecy of intelligence services. The secrecy of intelligence
apparatus and officials must be protected. Second, information
flow should not be interfered with or blocked by other agencies
or people. Intelligence products should be given directly to the
final consumer, in Russia, the president. Third, methods of
intelligence operations must be civilized. Blackmailing, pressure, or use of compromising materials should be avoided.
Fourth, national intelligence must remain non-partisan and be
freed from ideological and political bias. Fifth, intelligence
requirements must be depoliticized, and intelligence officers
should be able to work without political pressures. Finally, glas-

nost matters. The people are entitled to know what they pay taxes for to a certain degree. Selective opening of national intelligence is crucial not only for enhancing accountability, but also for winning public support.

Organizational Reforms: Centralization vs. Decentralization

Organizational reform of intelligence services was one of the most hotly debated subjects during the conference.[7] Two issues drew major attention. One involved pluralism in the intelligence community, and the other the separation of security and intelligence functions. Both issues were of great import and interest to the Korean audience since South Korea's intelligence community is characterized by a high degree of centralization. As chapter six demonstrates, the Agency for National Security Planning (ANSP) is the dominant intelligence agency in South Korea which combines foreign intelligence with domestic security and counter-espionage services. Other services such as the Defense Intelligence Agency, the National Military Security Command, and the National Police are minor actors. No pluralistic competition among intelligence and security services exists.[8]

Several Korean panelists and participants called for the

---

[7] For a recent debate on organizational reforms of intelligence service in United States, see James Q. Wilson, *Thinking about Reorganization* (Washington, D.C.: National Consortium on the Study of Intelligence, 1993).

[8] In the area of counter-espionage, there is a fierce competition among ANSP, military intelligence and security services, and the police. In foreign intelligence including North Korea, ANSP is the dominant actor by monopolizing access to the president.

decentralization of intelligence services. Concentration of power in a single agency has prevented the president from gaining access to more balanced and appropriate intelligence assessments and estimates. Pluralistic competition among intelligence agencies can produce more sound intelligence assessments. In light of Israeli experiences, Yaari also suggested the utility of a pluralistic intelligence community by offering a concrete example. Israel failed to come up with a proper early warning by the onset of the Yom Kipur War because of the monopolization of intelligence functions in the hands of Mosad. Had there been a more competitive intelligence environment, the Eyptian surprise attack could have been detected in advance. Likewise, pluralistic competition among intelligence agencies can bring about positive outcomes.

Several panelists pointed out that pluralism is not a panacea for the intelligence dilemma and warned that there are several pitfalls associated with the decentralization of intelligence services. It can precipitate inter-agency rivalry, loyalty competition, and the distorted flow of information.[9] Inter-agency coordination could be nightmarish. Apart from its entrophic pitfalls, decentralization could also lead to organizational expansion and increased resource needs. Thus, organizational reform for decentralization should be undertaken very prudently depending upon the overall security context and resource availability. A large country like the United States can easily adopt such a pluralistic system. It will be, however, very difficult for smaller countries with limited resource bases to adopt such a decentralized system.

---

[9] On the issue of coordination dilemma of pluralistic intelligence community, see a classic work by Irving Janis, *Groupthink* (Boston: Houghton-Mifflin, 1982).

As for the separation of foreign intelligence and domestic security functions, two divergent views have emerged. A great majority of Korean and foreign panelists argued for the separation. Colby, for example, directed our attention to the fact that all democratic countries separate their foreign intelligence from domestic security services. Foreign intelligence is by definition law-breaking since it involves covert actions, while domestic security services are designed to keep and enforce the law. Thus, two contradictory functions cannot be merged into a single organization. Although the U.S. has not been successful in coordinating foreign intelligence and domestic security services, the institutionalization of a good liasion between the two can resolve the coordination dilemma.

Korean panelists also supported the separation for different reasons. The merge of security and intelligence functions in the same organization has made ANSP too powerful.[10] Under past authoritarian regimes, the domestic security wing of ANSP deeply penetrated, controlled, and manipulated civil and political society for the purpose of regime security. Thus, domestic security and counter-espionage functions have been blamed for politicizing South Korea's intelligence service, undermining its accountability and public support, and eventually paralysing its proper functioning. Since the democratic opening in 1987, however, the South Korean government has made sweeping legal and institutional reforms of ANSP by banning its domestic political surveilance and interference. Its domestic security wing is now limited to counter-espionage, organized crimes,

---

[10] Despite major restructuring and change of its label, ANSP is on the historical continuum of the Korean Central Intelligence Agency (KCIA) whose institutional design was based on the integration of American CIA and FBI. KCIA under Park Chung-hee was notorious for misuse and abuse of its power for regime security. Its legacy still haunts the Korean people.

terrorism, and drug trafficking. Nevertheless, Korean panelists expressed concern since as long as two functions remain in the same organization, there is always high potential for its politicization.

A dissenting view was also echoed, however. The separation and/or integration of security and intelligence functions should be understood in the context of each country's specific internal and external environments. South Korea presents a unique case in this regard. Counter-espionage on North Korea's covert actions is inseparably intertwined with foreign intelligence operations, and vice versa. Other salient security issues such as organized crimes, terrorism, and drug trafficking all require intimate cooperation and coordination between the two. The separation of two functions will thus pose a major coordination dillema to South Korea's intelligence community. As Oliver Williamson argues, integration of the two functions into one organization might resolve the coordination dilemma by fostering the inflow of information and reducing transaction costs.[11] Furthermore, the separation would neither decentralize the power of the existing organization, nor economize human and financial resources. Organizational dynamics would create two giant services with overlapping functions and interests. Effective legislative oversight and executive control can easily prevent the politicization of ANSP and the abuse and misuse of its power.

---

[11] See Oliver E. Williamson, *The Economic Institutions of Capitalism* (New York: Free Press, 1985).

Intelligence Collection Methods:
HUMINT or Technical?

Utility and importance of technical intelligence was unanimously acknowledged. In this new age of diversified national security interests, expanded scope of intelligence requirements, and technological revolution, technical intelligence, both imagery and signal, represents a critical method of intelligence collection.[12] Its utility is particularly pronounced in the areas of political and military intelligence. Early warning capability now depends on the degree of sophistication of technical intelligence. Imagery intelligence can also be useful for economic and ecological security concerns. As a recent episode involving Japan-U.S. trade negotiations illustrates, signal intelligence can directly assist in enhancing economic security. Although the importance of technical intelligence is widely acknowledged, its actual adoption and implementation seems problematic. Only a few countries (e.g., U.S. Japan, and Russia), with enormous financial and technological capabilities, can effectively implement technical intelligence. Relatively speaking, it would be difficult for small and developing countries to engage in their own independent technical intelligence activities. They cannot afford to launch spy satellites, set up sophisticated electronic detection posts, or operate technical intelligence analysis functions. They are too expensive and too technologically overwhelming. A viable way to acquire technical intelligence is to rely on an ally

---

[12] See Jeffrey T. Richelson, *The American Intelligence Community* (Cambridge: Ballinger, 1988), pp. 145-231; J. T. Richelson, *Secret Eyes in Space* (Cambridge: Ballinger, 1990).

with such capability through intelligence cooperation. The case of U.S.-South Korean intelligence cooperation was cited in this context. However, Koreans were doubtful about the utility of such cooperation, not only because of Seoul's intelligence dependence on the U.S., but also because of the possibility of American manipulation of vital technical intelligence.

The growing importance of technical intelligence notwith-standing, panelists concurred with the idea that human intelli-gence (HUMINT) should remain as the backbone of national intelligence collection. Technical intelligence is a necessary, but insufficient condition for the effective functioning of national intelligence. It offers an accurate and comprehensive physical outlook, but fails to give finer pictures of intelligence targets. Such a gap should be made up for by human intelligence. In real situations, motives, intentions, and the will of key decision-makers can be more critical than physical details about military hardware and force movements. Thus, the human intelligence method should not be compromised. The issue at stake is how to improve effectiveness and to come up with more accurate and useful intelligence estimates.

The issue of covert actions also invited conflicting reactions from the panelists and audience.[13] During the Cold War period, covert actions, especially those by the U.S. and the Soviet Union, were pervasive, infringing on the soveriengty of other countries. Such activities were justified for the sake of national security. The rise of the post-hegemonic era has, however, posed fundamental domestic and external constraints to covert actions. Kirpitchenko explicitly pointed out that the Russian

---

[13] For a recent discussion of covert actions, see Roy Godson with Richard Kerr and Ernest May, *Covert Action in the 1990s* (Washington, D.C.: National Consortium on the Study of Intelligence, 1993).

Foreign Intelligence Service has suspended all forms of covert actions. However, the U.S. has not abandoned the use of covert actions. In the past, covert actions were designed to contest communist movements. But now, they are being utilized for other purposes such as cracking down international terrorist organizations and drug trafficking rings. Nevertheless, the U.S. has nowhere near the need for covert actions as it did during the Cold War. As the Iran-Contra scandal exemplifies, congressional oversight fundamentally limits the scope of covert actions. In view of the above, covert actions are still useful in some areas, but they are fundamentally constrained in many other ways.

Economic Intelligence: Myth and Reality

Just as economic security has emerged as an important national security agenda, economic intelligence too has attracted increasing attention from the public. Participants in the conference have also shown acute interest in the subject. However, discourses on economic intelligence have yielded diverse interpretations of its concepts, methods, and utilities. Some panelists argued that economic intelligence is nothing new. Many countries have long engaged in economic intelligence activities, especially involving military-industrial espionage and counter-economic espionage. Though different in degree for many countries, economic intelligence has constituted an important part of statecraft and national intelligence activities. Others have, however, asserted that in the post-Cold War era where economic competition has become more fierce, the old mode of economic intelligence is not enough. In the past, economic intelligence was by and large regarded as an instrument for enhancing military security, not economic security *per se*. For many countries, economic security has now become more pronounced than military security, and, therefore, priority in resource allocation should be given to the collection of economic intelligence.

The second major area of contestation involved the nature and scope of economic intelligence activities. Diversified and dynamic economic activities have made it difficult for national intelligence services to define targets of economic intelligence collection. For some countries, which adopt an explicit industrial and technological policy with specific strategtic targeting, what to collect becomes rather clear. Japan, France, and South Korea can be categorized in this group. To those countries devoid of such policies, however, targets and even the *raison d'etre* of economic intelligence become much more questionable. The U.S. presents a classical example in this regard. As Warner points out, however, economic intelligence is not confined to industrial and technological espionage. It can be useful in other areas. Counter-economic espionage activities offer an example. Intelligence services can also provide policy-makers with analyses of long-term economic trends, vital information on bilateral or multilateral trade negotiations, geopolitical implications of economic changes, political foundation of economic policy changes of major trading partners, and so on. Regarding all these issues, defining proper tasks of economic intelligence seems problematic.

Another issue concerns the distribution of economic intelligence. The collection of critical economic, industrial, and technological information is one thing, but their distribution is another. Who should be beneficiaries of the information collected? In democratic countries, economic intelligence is considered public goods since it is collected by tax-payers' money. Public goods cannot exclude or discriminate one beneficiary against other. Preferential allocation of such information would violate constitutional provisions, causing serious political backlash, and distorting maket mechanisms. Even for those countries that adopt explicit industrial targeting policies, distribution of economic intelligence can cause serious political problems. This is more so because it is virtually impossible to collect economic intelligence beneficial to every segment of society.

Finally, the utility of economic intelligence collection by national intelligence services has been questioned. Can intelligence services do well in collecting vital industrial and technological information? Several panelists were doubtful for at least two reasons. First, the life cycle of cutting-edge technology is shrinking, down to three-to-six months at best. It changes dynamically. By the time they collect and distribute, the information might become obsolete. This is more so because of bureaucratic red tape associated with distribution. Thus, it will be very difficult for intelligence officers, no matter how well trained, to collect updated economic intelligence and distribute it on a timely basis. Second, private firms could be much more efficient than national intelligence services. Several panelists such as Akio Kasai, Jang-hee Yoo, and Chung-min Lee pointed out that general trading companies in Japan and South Korea have global information networks broader than those of their national intelligence services and that their collection activities have been much more superior to those of the government sector. Even on the issue of counter-economic espionage, it was noted that private firms are better in guarding their own industrial and technological information than the government sector. Likewise, economic intelligence is an ambiguous entity which requires further analytical and empirical qualifications.

In addition to the issues raised above, several other pertinent themes were discussed throughout the conference. They include the quality of political leadership in controlling and steering intelligence services, the importance of winning public support, and the promotion of international intelligence cooperation. The quality of political leadership is critical because it eventually determines the structure, process, and performance of intelligence services. Poor and ill-informed leadership can bring about catastrophic effects on their performance and organizational survival. Democratic changes and the advent of a post-hegemonic world order can no longer justify the political insulation of intelligence services. They should win public support by performing well, being more accountable, and becoming more open to the public. Finally, international intelligence cooperation is vital to the maintenance of peace and stability in the world since it enhances transparency, certainty, and predictability. Intelligence cooperation has been particularly useful in stabilizing ethnic conflicts and fighting against organized crimes, international terrorism, and drug trafficking.

In view of the above, we can conclude that the coming of the new age has complicated the dimensions of national security and intelligence. The study of comparative national intelligence is facing new analytical, empirical, and policy frontiers. In this regard, a more systematic and cross-national comparison of intelligence services is more urgently needed than ever before.

Appendix

Intelligence Operations and Foreign Affairs*

Prof. Philip Vos Fellman

Readings

1. Codevilla, Angelo, *Informing Statecraft, Intelligence for a New Century*
2. Fellman, Philip, *Congress and the C.I.A.*
3. Gilligan, Tom, *CIA Life: 10,000 Days with the Agency.*
4. Godson, Roy, Ed. *Intelligence Requirements for the 1990's*
5. Ranelagh, John, *The Agency: The Rise and Decline of the C.I.A.*
6. Richelson, Jeffrey, *The U.S. Intelligence Community*
7. Stockwell, John, *In Search of Enemies*

Week I: Overview

A. Richelson, Chapter One, *Intelligence*, pp. 1-10.
Chapter Two, *National Intelligence Organizations*, pp.

---

* Department of Political Science, Yale University.

11-34.

B. Fellman, Chapter One, *Intelligence policy and Public Policy*, pp. 1-66.

C. Codevilla, Chapter One, *The Nature and Importance of Intelligence*, pp. 3-47.

Chapter Two, *New World Disorder*, pp. 48-72.

Week II: The Historical Origins of the C.I.A.

A. Ranelagh, Chapter One, *Cruel Necessity*, pp. 37-56.

Chapter Two, *In the Service of A Republic*, pp. 57-92.

Chapter Three, *Fear and Emergency*, pp. 93-111.

Chapter Four, *Dawn Like Thunder*, pp. 112-142.

Chapter Five, *Double Trouble*, pp. 143-159.

Chapter Six, *Among the Ruins*, pp. 160-190.

or:

B. Fellman, Chapter Two, *Central Intelligence During the Cold War*, pp. 67-114.

and:

C. Gilligan, *Introduction*, pp. 1-12.

Chapter One, *Getting Hired*, pp. 13-24.

Chaper Two, *CIA in History*, pp. 25-44

Chapter Three, *Getting Started, Getting Trained*, pp. 45-58.

Chapter Four, *The Bay of Pigs*, pp. 59-66

Chapter Five, *Preparing for Assignment Abroad*, pp. 67-76.

Chapter Six, *Assignment in El Dorado*, pp. 77-100.

Week III: The Intelligence Cycle

A. Codevilla, Chapter Three, *Vain Spying*, pp. 75-129.

Chapter Four, *Fragmented Counterspying*, pp. 130-186.

B. Godson, Chapter One, *Intelligence for the 1990's,* pp. 1-30.
Chapter Two, *Collection,* pp. 31-70.

Week IV: Intelligence Analysis

A. Godson, Chapter Three, *Analysis,* pp. 71-126.
B. Richelson, Chapter Thirteen, *Analysis and Estimates,* pp. 289-316.
C. Codevilla, Chapter Five, Getting It Wrong, pp. 187-239.

Week V: Intelligence Operations: The History

A. Ranelagh, Chapter Seven, *Terra Nostra,* pp. 190-228.
Chapter Eight, *The Wounded Peace,* pp. 229-269.
Chapter Nine, *Cry Havoc,* pp. 270-309.
Chapter Ten, *Planes, Plans and Plots,* pp. 310-348.
B. Gilligan, Chapter Seven, *Back Inside,* pp. 101-110.
Chapter Eight, *CIA and Chile,* pp. 111-132.
Chapter Nine, *Assignment to Zaragossa,* pp. 133-146.
C. Codevilla, Chapter Six, *Sorcerers' Apprentices,* pp. 240-274.

Film: Yuri Nosenko: KGB

One Page Term Paper Abstracts Due

Week VI: Intelligence Failure: From the Bay of Pigs to Vietnam

A. Fellman, Chapter Three, *Central Intelligence 1961-72: The Decline of an Empire,* pp. 115-158.

B. Ranelagh, Chapter Eleven, *On the Beach,* pp. 349-382.
Chapter Twelve, *Touch Football,* pp. 383-426.
Chapter Thirteen, *Agency Agonistes,* pp. 427-478.
C. Gilligan, Chapter Ten, *Deep Cover Doldrums,* pp. 147-158.
Chapter Eleven, *Turbulent Times for CIA,* pp. 159-172.
Chapter Twelve, *Headhunting and Beancounting,* pp. 173-192.
Chapter Thirteen, *The Farm Revisited,* pp. 193-206.
Chapter Fourteen, *Casey Comes to Town,* pp. 207-220.
Chapter Fifteen, *Covert Action Charade,* pp. 221-230.

Week VII: Congressional Control of Intelligence

A. Fellman, Chapter Four, *The C.I.A. Under Fire,* pp. 159-199.
Chapter Five, *The Battle Continues,* pp. 200-253.
B. Ranelagh, Chapter Fourteen, *On The Edge,* pp. 479-509.
Chapter Fifteen, *The President's Men?,* pp. 510-544.
Chapter Sixteen, *Power Plays: 1972-76,* pp. 545-583.
C. Gilligan, Chapter Sixteen, *In the Open,* pp. 231-244.
Chapter Seventeen, *CIA and the Threats Facing America in the 1990's,* pp. 245-258.

Film: No Way Out

Week VIII: Congress, The President and the C.I.A.

A. Fellman, Chapter Six, *Executive Order 11905 and the Permanent Oversight Committees,* pp. 254-297.
B. Ranelagh, Chapter Seventeen, *Survival, 1974-76,* pp. 584-626.
Chapter Eighteen, *Secrecy in the Republic,* pp. 627-655.

Week IX: Covert Action Disaster

Week X: Managing Intelligence

Week XI: Covert Conflicts in Foreign Policy

A. Codevilla, Chapter Eleven, *Subversion and Policy*, pp. 355-386.
B. Stockwell, Chapter Ten, *Advisors, Technicians and Foreign Troops*, pp. 176-190.
Chapter Eleven, *Propaganda and Politics*, pp. 191-202.
Chapter Twelve, *Business and Money*, pp. 203-212.
Chapter Thirteen, *Disaster*, pp. 213-226.
Chapter Fourteen, *CIA vs. Congress*, pp. 227-239.
Chapter Fifteen, *Disengagement*, pp. 240-248.
Chapter Sixteen, *Postscript*, pp. 249-254.

Week XII: Continuing Problems

A. Codevilla, Chapter Twelve, *Getting It Right*, pp. 387-438.
B. Richelson, Chapter Nineteen, *Issues*, pp. 441-455.
C. Fellman and Colby, (Handout) *Future Intelligence*, pp. i-xiv.

Week XIII: Conclusion—Intelligence and the Future

A. Codevilla, Chapter Thirteen, *Intelligence, Talent and lessons*, pp. 440-449.
B. Fellman and Janda, (Handout) *Intelligence and the Constitution*, pp. 1-28.

Intelligence and Covert Operations*

Prof. H. Bradford Westerfield

Intelligence and covert operations are important, interesting, and intellectually challenging. And there is now enough information in the public domain to study them seriously. This course aims to do so for the period since the end of World War II. It aims to be as relevant to the post-Cold War era as possible, and to pay attention to the intelligence work of Britain, Israel, and Japan—but the availability of English-language material necessitates that the main emphasis be upon exemplifying intelligence and covert operations in the global struggle between the United States and Russia during the Cold War.

The format is straight lectures, three times a week. Depending on the size of the class, student questions will be welcomed during the lectures—and at least after them and in office hours and during review-sessions that will be held before each exam. There will be two exams: a midterm take home exam and a 2 1/2-hour final. Reading assignments are lengthy during the first half of the course, somewhat shorter during the second half, to allow time for a 4000-

---

* Department of Political Science, Yale University.

6000 word term paper, due at the beginning of the Reading Period. Many topic options will be offered, with readings suggested for each option; so the task is not to seek out sources but to provide synthesis and analysis. (True research papers on other relevant subjects may be acceptable through consultation with Mr. Westerfield.)

So that students can share the books for the papers without conflict, an aim is to have all the books for all the paper-topic options put on 3-day reserve by the beginning of March, in time for work on the papers to start.

The required reading assignments are for purchase at the Co-op or in "professors' packets" at TYCO's.

The weighting of the course grade will be 1/4 for the midterm take-home exam, 3/8 for the paper, and 3/8 for the final exam, which will be mostly on the second half of the course.

Readings and lectures are designed to complement not duplicate each other. Both exams will be entirely essay questions, with about equal emphasis on the readings and the lectures overall (each individual question will bear on readings and lectures but not necessarily in equal proportions question-by-question). Questions commonly aim for fresh thinking, not just for regurgitation; but familiarity with the main themes (and major examples, though not the picky details) of readings and lectures is expected. Students must learn to read the course-assigned books swiftly with that in mind.

A much more detailed (30 page) version of this syllabus will be available soon as a TYCO's packet, including hundreds of book citations, broken down mostly as appropriate for particular suggested term-paper topics. These titles will help you decide on a topic (at the end of February), as well as guide you about the one you do decide on.

Meanwhile this syllabus gives the basics about the course,

which is organized not chronologically but according to the various functional categories of intelligence and covert operations.

Note that the dates indicated for lectures and readings in each part of the course are not the same. This is to show you how to spread the readings most evenly and appropriately and not fall behind.

1. Overview
Lectures Jan. 11-Feb. 8. / **Readings** Jan. 11-27.

Thomas Powers, *The Man Who Kept the Secrets: Richard Helms and the CIA*, pp. v-xv, 3-69, 73-165, 200(line 13)-201, 220-307. (The most perceptive history of CIA, up to 1977).

Christopher Andrew and Oleg Gordievsky, *KGB: The Inside Story*. All of it is good, but the following pagination reduces it to reasonable required length, principally by deleting the parts that predate World War II and those on Eastern Europe since that war. So the assignment is pp. 1-16, 173-232, 279-330, 349-351 top, 367-381 top, 389-404, 422-427, 435-462, 469 ft.-481 top, 495-514, 524 ft.-531, 541-593, 597 mid.-619.

Related term-paper topics:
British intelligence activities.
Canadian intelligence activities.
Israeli intelligence activities.

2. Technical Collection of Intelligence ("TECHINT"), and Technical Countermeasures
Lectures Feb. 10. / **Readings** Jan. 28-Feb. 8.

TYCO's packet: The techint items.
Clifford Stoll, *The Cuckoo's Egg: Tracking a Spy through the Maze of Computer Espionage*, entire.
Related term-paper topics:

Recent technology and prospects.

A compartive case study of two U-2 spy-plane crises: the 1960 shootdown and the Cuba missile crisis.

The 1968-69 Pueblo seizure and EC-121 shootdown affairs, and case studies.

The 1979 "discovery" of Russian troops in Cuba, as a case study.

The 1983 Korean airline shootdown affair, as a case study. (Here alternative concentrations could be upon determining what the two sides did or upon ethically evaluating it.)

3. Espionage ("HUMINT")

Lectures Feb. 12-24. / **Reading** Feb. 9-23.

Jerrold L. Schechter and Peter Deriabin, *The Spy Who Saved the World* [Oleg Penkovsky], pp. 439-441, xii-xvi, i-421.

Related term-paper topics. Those that are marked also apply to counterespionage #5 below.

- Selected aspects of the tradecraft.
- High technology as the means of humint and counterespionage.
- High technology as the targets of humint; also the pertinent counterintelligence competition.
- Comparing cases of case-officer/agent relationships.
- Renegades. Case studies.

  Humint and covert action in Europe in the first half of the Cold War.

  Espionage arising from "countercultures" in Britain, Russia, and the United States.

  The Walker-family spy case.

  The Pollard case of Israeli espionage in the United States.

- Penetration and counterpenetration in Moscow in the 1980s: Some interpretations of CIA and KGB efforts.

Feb. 26. Take-Home Exam due, on readings and class material to this date.

4. The Functioning of Analysis and Estimates, vis-a-vis Policymaking

Lectures Feb. 26-March 22. / **Readings** Feb. 27-March 5.

David Kennedy, *Sunshine and Shadow: CIA and the Soviet Economy,* entire.

TYCO's packet: Articles by Richard K. Betts.

Related term-paper topics:

Deception operations.

Analysis relations between Washington and overseas stations.

The interplay between strategic and tactical intelligence analysis in the Lebanese crises, 1982-84.

Comparison of U.S. disputes between analysts and policymakers—about Israeli nuclear weapons development, the 1968 Tet offensive in Vietnam, and the 1983 Korean airliner shootdown.

5. Counterespionage

Lectures March 24-April 7. / **Readings** March 6-24.

Tom Mangold, *Cold Warrior: James Jesus Angleton, The CIA's Master Spy Hunter,* entire.

Related term-paper topics, besides those marked under #3 Espionage above.

Conspiracies in President Kennedy's assassination and/or in those of Martin Luther King, Jr., and Robert Kennedy?

Moles in Canada.

6. Conducting Covert Action: (a) With Paramilitary Operations, or (b) Without Them ("Political Action")

Lectures April 9-18. / **Readings** March 25-April 10.

Pat Choate, *Agents of Influence* (Japan's penetration of the U.S.), pp. 19 top-20 mid., 22 mid.-34, 36-41 mid., 49-63, 70-214.

Andrew and Leslie Cockburn, *Dangerous Liaison: The Inside Story of the U.S.—Israeli Covert Relationship,* pp. 1-70, 98-345.

Margaret E. Scranton, *The Noriega Years: U.S.-Panamanian Relations,* 1981-1990, pp. 8-14, 49-152 (of this, 49-73 may be just skimmed), 44 ft.-46, 41-43, 153-212.

Related term-paper topics:

Proprietaries (cover companies). Case studies.

Agents-of-influence and lobbyists for foreigners. Case studies.

Propaganda and cultural relations, under cover. Case studies.

Some cases of the Soviet bloc's deception operations.

U.S. involvement in coups d'etat. Comparison of Iran (1953), Equador (1960-63), Indonesia (1964-66), and Chile (1970-73). Or substitute Vietnam (Diem, 1963) for one of these.

CIA and the coups in Greece (1965-68).

The overthrow of Allende in Chile (1970-73).

The assassination of Allende's former foreign minister, Letelier, by rightists in Washington(1976).

Covert action in Syria and Lebanon in the 1950s.

U.S. covert action and the founding of the Diem regime in South Vietnam (1954-56).

U.S. covert action and the overthrow of the Diem regime in South Vietnam (1963).

Undercover support for Tibetan rebellions against commuist China in the 1950s and 1960s.

Zaire (formerly the Belgian Congo) in the 1960s.

Comparison of the Guatemala invasion (1953-54) and the Bay of Pigs (1960-61).

OPERATION MONGOOSE against Castro after the Bay of Pigs.

7. Controlling Covert Action Especially When It Includes Paramilitary Operations

Lectures Apr. 21.

No reading assignment, to allow time for your paper.

Related term-paper topics:

Counterinsurgency in Vietnam and Laos. (A number of sub-options for papers).

The Nicaraguan Contras.

The Iran/Contra affair.

Angola in the 1970s and 1980s.

Any one of the following comparisons:

Nicaragua-Guatemala.

Nicaragua-Bay of Pigs.

Nicaragua-Tibet.

Angola-Guatemala.

Angola-Bay of Pigs.

Angola-Tibet.

Nicaragua-OPERATION MONGOOSE.

The abortive Iranian hostage rescue mission.(1979-80).

A comparision of that and the also unsuccessful Son Tay mission in Vietnam to rescue U.S. prisoners of war.

Paramilitary operations and the problems of becoming preoccupied with avoiding possible leaks: Comparison of the Bay of Pigs and the Iranian hostage rescue mission.

Cases of zealots in covert action and paramilitary operations.

Cases of renegades.

The ethics of assassination as an instrument of state policy, with special (but not exclusive) attention to the U.S. plots and to possible Oswald-Cuba-USSR connections about President Kennedy.

The possible applicability of the "doctrine of just war" in ethical evaluations of covert operations.

Countering international terrorism.

CIA's psychiatric experiments with durgs.

CIA, the Drug Enforcement Administration (DEA), and drug dealers.

Congressional oversight.

8. "Domestic Counterintelligence" (or "Internal Security"); Countering Domestic Dissidence and Resistance

Lecture Apr. 23. / **Readings** Apr. 22-23.

Richard Gid Powers, *Secrecy and Power: The Life of J. Edgar Hoover*, pp. 1-20, 28-38 mid., 55-73, 89-91, 94-100 top, 122 ft.-131, 140-143, 146 ft.-158, 161-164 mid., 169-180, 209-239, 251-257, 275-311, 316-332, 336 mid.-383, 391-480, 486-492.

Ross Gelbspan, *Break-Ins, Death Threats, and the FBI*, pp. 1-215.

Related term-paper topics:

Controlling domestic counterintelligence.

The (Senator) McCarthy era of the 1950s.

The FBI's surveillance/harassment/disruption programs (especially COMINPIL and COINTELPRO) against any one of the following or any combination thereof:

The Communist party.

The Socialist Workers party.

The Black Panthers party and other Black Nationalists.

Martin Luther King. Jr.

The New Left and the peace movement.

CIA's OPERATION CHAOS against the New Left in America.

(These topics on domestic counterintelligence, and some others on the syllabus, e.g. CIA's psychiatric experiments with drugs, may lend themselves to papers carefully emphasizing ethical considerations—but not just to flights of rhetoric.)

The Role of Intelligence in International Security*

Prof. Harold Scott

This course examines the role of intelligence in international security. Although much of the material in the course refers to the U.S., the course is comparative in scope. Specifically, we will explore how nations organize the tasks of intelligence community: collection, intelligence analysis, counterintelligence, and covert operations. We will place considerable emphasis on the intelligence-policy nexus, particularly as it pertains to how and why intelligence failures occur.

Although there are no formal prerequisites for this course, familiarity with bureaucratic processes and the decisionmaking literature will help.

Requirements

This course places a heavy emphasis on student participation.

---

* Graduate School of Public and International Affairs, University of Pittsburgh.

Participation is defined both in terms of a students familiarity with the assigned readings and in their willingness to involve themselves in class discussions. There are three basic components to the course grade:

- class participation 33%.
- three papers 7-14 pages 33%.
- a 20-30 minute class presentation 33%.

I will assign each student his/her topic for the 20-30 minute presentation. You will be required to write a paper on this assigned topic, due the last day of the semester. The other two papers you have a choice, but I will expect these papers on the day we discuss the particular topic (i.e. covert operations papers are due Week 14, Counterintelligence Week 13 etc.) Absolutely no exceptions!

Readings: There are three recommended books for purchase.

James Bamford, *The Puzzle Palace.*
Dan Raviv and Yossi Melman, *Every Spy a Prince.*
Abram Shulsky, *Silent Warfare: Understanding the World of Intelligence.*

All other assigned readings are on reserve in the library, if not please notify me immediately.

Week 1: Introduction

Part I) What is Intelligence?

Week 2: The nature of Intelligence: Science or Art?

Walter Laqueur, *A World of Secrets : The Uses and Limits of Intelligence*, Chapters 3-4 & 10.

Abram Shulsky, *Silent Warfare: Understanding the World of Intelligence*, Chapters 1, 7-8.

Ernest May, *Knowing One's Enemies: Intelligence Assessment Before the Two World Wars*.

Ernest May, "Conclusions: Capabilities and Proclivities."

Week 3: The Assessment Problem: Does Intelligence produce?

Ernest May, "Cabinet, Tsar, Kaiser: Three Approaches to Assessment;"Michael Geyer, "National Socialist Germany: The Politics of Information;" Michael Barnhart, "Japanese Intelligence before the Second World War: 'Best Case' Analysis;" and David Kahn, "United States Views of Germany and Japan in 1941;" in Ernest May ed., *Knowing One's Enemies*.

Part II) Intelligence and Security: A Common Problem?

Week 4: The Allies

Jeffery Richelson, *Foreign Intelligence Organizations*, Chapters 2, 3, 6, & 8.

Week 5: The Soviet Union

John Dziak, *Chekisty: History of the KGB*.

Week 6: Israel

Daniel Ravi, and Yossi Melman, *Every Spy a Prince.*

Week 7: The United States

Charles Ameringer, *U.S. Foreign Intelligence; The Secret Side of American History,* pp. 17-87.
Thomas Powers, *The Man Who Kept the Secrets,* pp. 28-62, 71-87.
Henry Howe Ransom, "Secret Intelligence in the United State, 1947-1982: The CIA's Search for Legitimacy." in Christopher Andrew and David Dilks, *The Missing Dimension: Governments and Intelligence Communities in the Twentieth Century.*

Part III) The Elements of Intelligence

Week 8: Collection

Cord Meyer, "The Collectors," in *Facing Reality: From World Federalism to the CIA.*
Abram Shulsky, *Silent Warfare: Understanding the World of Intelligence,* Chapter 2.
Roy Godson, *Intelligence Requirements for the 1990s: Collection and Analysis.*
Counterintelligence and Covert Action, Collection.

Week 9: Technical Collection

James Bamford, *The Puzzle palace.*

Week 10: Intelligence and policy

Willmoore Kendall, "The Functions of Intelligence," *World Politics* I

(July 1949): pp. 543-552.

Thomas Hughes, *The Fate of Facts in a World of Men.*

Arthur S. Hulnick, "The Intelligence Producer-Policy Consumer Linkage: A Theoretical Approach." in *Intelligence and National Security*, vol. 1, no. 2, May 1986.

L. Keith Gardiner, "Squaring the Circle: Dealing with Intelligence-Policy Breakdowns," *Intelligence and National Security*, vol. 6, 1 (1991).

Week 11: Intelligence Analysis

Abram Shulsky, *Silent Warfare: Understanding the World of Intelligence*, pp. 37-59.

Roy Godson, *Intelligence Requirements for the 1990s: Collection and Analysis, Counterintelligence and Covert Action*, Chapter 3.

Roy Godson, *Intelligence Requirements for the 1980s: Analysis and Estimates*, Chapters 3 and 5.

Richard Pipes, "Team B: The Reality Behind the Myth." *Commentary* 82(October 1986) 25-40.

Week 12: Intelligence Failure

Abram Shulsky, *Silent Warfare: Understanding the World of Intelligence*, pp. 59-72.

Richard Betts, "Analysis, War and Decision: Why Intelligence Failures are Inevitable," in *World Politics*, XXXI (October 1978).

Michael Handel, "Technological Surprise and War," *Intelligence and National Security* (May 1986), 255-271.

Robert M. Blum, "Surprised by Tito: The Anatomy of an Intelligence Failure," *Diplomatic History*, pp. 39-57.

Week 13: Counterintelligence

Abram Shulsky, *Silent Warfare: Understanding the World of Intelligence,* Chapter 5.

Roy Godson, *Intelligence Requirements for the 1980s: Counterintelligence,* Chapters 2, 5, & 9.

Arnold Beichman, "Can Counterintelligence Come in from the Cold?" *Policy Review* 15 (Winter 1981), pp. 93-101.

Tom Polgar, "Defection and Redefection," in *International Journal of Intelligence and Counterintelligence,* 1(1986), pp. 29-44.

Barton Whaley, "Toward a General Theory of Deception."*Journal of Strategic Studies* 5 (March 1982).

Week 14: Covert Operations

Abram Shulsky, *Silent Warfare: Understanding the World of Intelligence,* Chapter 4.

Roy Cline, "Covert Action is Needed for United States Security," in Don Mansfield and Gary.

Buckley, *Conflict in American Foreign Policy.*

Theodore Shackley, "The Third Option," *Readers Digest Press* 1981.

Richard Fak, "CIA Covert Action and International Law," *Society*
· 12 (March/April 1975).

Week 15: Intelligence and Democracy

Abram Shulsky, *Silent Warfare: Understanding the World of Intelligence,* Chapter 6.

Winston S. Churchill, *Marlborough: His Life and Times,* vol. 6, pp. 482-484 and 526-529.

Additional Readings TBA.

Comparative Intelligence Systems*

Prof. Myles Robertson

Students must answer EITHER question one OR two and THREE others

1. Does the creation of models, such as the "intelligence cycle," contribute greatly to understanding the relationship between an intelligence community, policymakers and the foreign policy-making process?

or

2. What is the proper role for intelligence in the foreign policy process?
3. To what extent is the term "intelligence community" a misnomer? Discuss with reference to various national examples.
4. "The funcitioning of intelligence agencies and their relationship to government can best be understood through the study of bureaucratic theory." Discuss.
5. Why do small states, such as Canada and Australia, with limited

---

* Department of International Relations, University of St. Andrews, Scotland, U.K.

foreign policy objectives have seemingly significant intelligence communities?

6. Are intelligence failures indicative of anything? Discuss with reference to at least FOUR case studies.

7. Covert action is a less useful foreign policy tool today than it was twenty years ago. Discuss.

8. What are the inherent tensions between democratic government and the requirements of operating an effective intelligence community?

9. "The best defence against terrorism is good intelligence". Discuss.

10. How do you think intelligence and its roles will be affected by the existence of the 'post cold war world'?

Comparative Intelligence Systems

Comparative intelligence systems is a course which sets out to examine the relationship, in various Western countries, between their 'foreign intelligence gathering and assessment' agencies and the making and implementing of foreign and national security policies. It is a course about how information and intelligence play a role in decision-making processes. It considers the problems involved in analysing factors in international politics for the purposes of producing coherent national foreign and defence policy.

The course is composed of three sections. The first section provides the analytical core of the course and sets out the various ideas, models and concepts on how, and in what ways, intelligence agencies and their product contribute—and should contribute—to foreign policy making. The second section examines each respective country's foreign intelligence agencies and how they fit into the policy process, structure and organisation. The third section comprises a series of case studies which examine the relationship between the agencies, policymaking and policymakers in practice and shows how agencies have contributed to, and moulded, national security policy in particular issues.

The idea behind a course which is "comparative," aside from providing as broad a picture as possible, is to try to highlight how countries which are superficially similar i.e. western democracies with similar attendant value systems, approach the whole question of intelligence—its uses and its management, its advantages and its problems—from often very different perspectives. One of the objectives is to highlight how different national solutions have been adopted for what are often transnational intelligence-related phenomena.

Course Requirements: Students are required to complete three essays—one per term—which will serve as the appropriate seminar discussion paper. These essays will be of a maximum 2,500 words in length. All essays must be typewritten. Students are also required to complete a 500 word book review of a book selected from a topic other than their essay subjects. The teaching schedule will be interrupted in the middle of each term by a 'reading week' when there will be no formal classes and students are expected to utilise the time as an opportunity for wider reading.

Note on Sources and Material

The subject matter of this course is a recognised—if not widespread—area of enquiry within academic institutions and policy-related organisations. This is so particularly in the United States, less so in the United Kingdom and also takes place to a limited extent in Australia and Canada. Four disciplines, with their focus on different aspects, have made the major contributions to the field: these are Political Science, International Relations, Modern History and Law. Thus, though a specialised area, there is a reasonably wide range of high quality material available.

However, given the subject nature, there is also available a larger body of further source material. This is of highly variable quality. It ranges from e.g. valuable personal memoirs, through what might be generously termed journalism of mass popular appeal to the highly critical 'expose genre' which often (but not always) has been written by individuals with some particular 'axe to grind'. Much of this second category of material is not 'worthless' : but its limitations (and dangers) do have to be recognised. Therefore when utilising such sources these points must be borne in mind in order to arrive at a balanced judgement and separate fact, fiction, misinformation, disinformation and straightforward lies.

For a useful overview of these issues students should read: Rusbridger, *The Intelligence Game*(Chapter 8 'Telling the Tale'); Lowenthal, M., 'The Intelligence Library: Quality vs. Quantity' *INS* Vol. 2 No. 2 April 1987; Hunter, D., 'Evolution of Literature on US Intelligence' *AFS* Fall 1978.

The material in the course guide has been arranged to serve various purposes. Primary and secondary sources have been indicated. Suggested reading for topics has been organised to provide as wide a range of sources as possible but also to indicate the range of component issues/subject areas which should at least be mentioned (if not dealt with at length) in any essay coverage of that particular topic.

Students should note that the topics are often inter-related. Reading lists on particular topics have been organised as such quite often for ease of presentation and manageability. Therefore a comprehensive answer to one particular issue question will require a balanced integration of material/ideas from many different topics.

Primary reading has been indicated with an asterisk.*

Abbreviations for major journal material cited in the reading list are

AFS	Armed Forces and Society
APSR	American Political Science Review
CHR	Canadian Historical Review
CQ	Conflict Quarterly (Canada)
DH	Diplomatic History
DIJ	Defense Intelligence Journal (Defense Intelligence College, U.S.)
EIA	Ethics In International Affairs
FA	Foreign Affairs
FP	Foreign Policy
FSJ	Foreign Service Journal (US State Department)
GLJ	Georgetown Law Journal
HJ	Historical Journal
IA	International Affairs
IJIC	International Journal of Intelligence and Counterintelligence
INS	Intelligence and National Security
IS	International Security
ISQ	International Studies Quarterly
JILP	Journal of International Law and Politics
JLS	Journal of Law and Society
JMAS	Journal of Modern African Studies
JSS	Journal of Strategic Studies
LSQ	Legislative Studies Quarterly (US Congress)
ORBIS	

PARAMETERS   (US Army War College)
POLITY
PL   Public Law
PS   Political Science
PSQ   Political Studies Quarterly
RUSI   Royal United Services Institute
SEPR   South Eastern Political Review (United States)
SR   Strategic Review
TPQ   The Political Quarterly
USAPS   US Academy of Political Science
UTLJ   University of Toronto Law Journal
WP   World Politics
WQ   Washington Quarterly

Material with an (+) can be found in the RISCT library.

Defining the Field

The subject matter of the coures is a specialised and thus unfa-
miliar field. In order that the basic structure and terminology be
understood students at some point should endeavour to read relevant sections of:

Godson, R., (ed) *Intelligence Requirements for the 1980s: Vols, 1-5 and 7*

_____ *Elements of Intelligence*
_____ *Analysis and Estimates*
_____ *Counterintelligence*
_____ *Covert Action*

_____ *Clandestine Collection*
_____ *Intelligence and Policy*
_____ *Intelligence Requirements for the 1990s: Collection, Analysis, Counterintelligence and Covert Action*

As general introductory guides and all-course texts students should also consult

A. Shulsky, *Silent Warfare: Understanding the World of Intelligence*
A. Bozeman, *Strategic Intelligence and Statecraft: Selected Essays*
W. Laquer, *A World of Secrets: The Uses and Limits of intelligence*
A. Maurer et al., *Intelligence: Policy and Process*

and as a general compendium text should utilise

Harold P. Ford, *Estimative Intelligence: The purposes and Problems of National Intelligence Estimating*

Policy, Organisation and Theory

The material listed below establishes the theories, models and concepts which delineate the role and function of 'intelligence' in relation to the making and implementing of foreign and security policy.

These ideas and concepts are applicable to all topics/questions and should be utilised accordingly. Students should use the ideas and issues raised by this reading as the basis for analysis of course topics e.g. the citations by Ben-lsrael, Herman, Garthoff (among others) are all pertinent to understanding the issues and problems in the later topic on US intelligence estimates of the Soviet strategic threat.

Question 1 *Is there such a thing as an 'intelligence cycle'? If so, how does it work?*

Question 2 *What role should intelligence play in formulating foreign and defence policy. Are there any problems associated with this task?*

Armstrong, A., 'Bridging the Gap: Intelligence and Policy' *WQ* Winter 1989

Ben-Israel, I., 'Philosophy and Method of Intelligence: The Logic of the Estimate Process' *INS* October 1989*

Betts, R. 'Intelligence for Policy Makers' *WQ* Summer 1980*

Betts, R., 'Strategic intelligence Estimates' *Parameters* Vol. 10 1980

Betts, R., 'Policymakers and Intelligence Analysts' *INS* Vol. 3 January 1988*

Bozeman, A., 'Statecraft and Intelligence in the Non-Western World' *Conflict* No. 6 1985

Brammer, D., Hulnick, A., 'Intelligence and Policy-The Ongoing Debate' *SII* Winter 1980

Bruce Lockhart, J., 'The Relationship between Secret Services and Government in a Modern State' *RUSI* March 1974

Central Intelligence Agency, *Intelligence: The Acme of Skill*

Central Intelligence Agency, *Fact Book On Intelligence*

Cimbala, S., (ed.) *Intelligence and Intelligence Policy in a Democratic State*

Cline, R., 'Policy Without intelligence' *FP* Winter 1974-75

Gardiner, L. 'Squaring the Circle: Dealing With Intelligence-Policy Breakdowns' *INS* Vol. 6 January 1991 No. 1*

Garthoff, R., 'Estimating and Imputing Intentions' *IS* Winter 1978

Gazit, S., 'Intelligence Estimates and the Decision-maker' *INS* Vol. 3 No. 3 July 1988*

Godson, R., *Intelligence Requirements for the 1990s*

Handel, M., (ed.) *Leaders and Intelligence* (all except Chapters 2 and

3)

Handel, M., *War, Strategy and Intelligence* (Part 2: Intelligence and Strategy)

Handel, M., 'The Politics of Intelligence' *INS* October 1987*

Handel, M., 'Leaders and Intelligence' *INS* Vol. 3 No. 3 July 1988

Herman, M., 'Intelligence and Assessment of Military Capability: Reasonable Sufficiency or Worst Case?' *INS* Vol. 4 No. 4 October 1989*

Herman, M., 'Intelligence and Policy: A Comment' *INS* Vol. 6 No. 1 January 1991*

Hilsman, R., 'On Intelligence' *AFS* Fall 1981

Hilsman, R., 'Intelligence and Policymaking in Foreign Affairs' *WP* Vol. 5 1952

Hulnick, A. 'Managing Intelligence Analysis' *IJIC* Vol. 2 No. 3 1988

Hulnick, A., 'The Intelligence Producer-Policy Consumer Linkage' *INS* Vol. 1 May 1986*

Jervis, R., 'What's Wrong With The intelligence Process?' *IJIC* Spring 1986

Jervis, R., 'Intelligence and Foreign Policy' *IS* Winter 1986-87

Johnson, L., 'Making the intelligence Cycle Work' *IJIC* Winter 1986-87*

Johnson, L., 'Strategic Intelligence: An American Perspective' *IJIC* Fall 1989

Johnson, L., 'Decision Costs in the intelligence Cycle' *JSS* Vol. 7 1984

Jones, R. *Reflections On Intelligence*

Jones, R., 'Intelligence and Command' *INS* Vol. 3 No. 3 July 1988

Kent, S., 'Estimates and Influence' *FSJ* April 1969

Hochsrema, R., 'The Presidential Role in Insuring Efficient, Economical and Responsible Intelligence Services' *PSQ* No. 8 1979

Hopple, G., Watson, B., *The Military Intelligence Community**

Johnson, L., *America's Secret Power: The CIA In A Democratic Society*

Johnson, L., 'Intelligence Policy in the Carter and Reagan Administrations' *SEPR* Vol. 16 1988

Kent, S., *Strategic Intelligence For American World Policy*

Kirkpatrick, L., *US Intelligence: Foreign Policy and Domestie Activities*

Melbourne, R., 'Odyssey of the NSC' *SR* Summer 1983

Prados, J., *The Keepers of the Keys: A History of the National Security Council From Truman to Bush*

Presidential Documents, *United States Intelligence Activities: Executive Order 12036 24 January 1978*

Presidential Documents, *United States Intelligence Activities: Executive Order 12333 4 December 1981*

Quirk, P., *Readinge On The Intelligence Community*

Ranelagh, J., *The Agency: The Rise and Decline of the CIA*

Richelson, J., *The US intelligence Community*

Ruhl, R., 'Intelligence Policy and Performance in Reagan's First term' *IJIC* Vol. 4 No. 1 Spring 1990*

Simmons, R., 'Intelligence Policy and Performance in Reagan's First term: A Good Record or Bad?' *IJIC* Spring 1990*

Smith, R., *The Unknown CIA*

Thomas, S., 'On the Selection of Directors of Central Intelligence' *SEPR* Vol. 9 1981

Turner, M., 'Understanding CIA's Role in Intelligence' *IJIC* Fall 1990*

US Congress, Select Committee on Intelligence, *Intelligence and Policy*

Volkman E., Blagett, B., *Secret Intelligence: America's Espionage Empire*

Woodward, B., *Veil: The Secret Wars of the CIA 1981-1987*

Apart from material cited above which deals with overall perspectives on issues, students should consult relevant secondary US material from other topic lists.

Further to this there is a range of more specialised US material e.g. US Congressional reports, which are available from me.

The United Kingdom

Question *Estimate the role that the British Intelligence Community has played in post war British foreign policy. Illustrate your answer with some specific examples.*

Aldrich, R., (ed.) *British Intelligence. Strategy and the Cold War 1945-1951**

Andrew, C., 'Whitehall, Washington and the Intelligence Services' *IA* July 1977

Charles, D., 'Sir Maurice Oldfield and British Intelligence: Some Lessons for Canada?' *CQ* Vol. 2 1982

Charlton, M., *Sailing Without An Anchor—The American Constitution and the Rise of the President's Men* Part 5 (BBC Radio Transcript)

Dickie, J., *Inside the Foreign Office*

Dorril, S., *The Silent Conspiracy: Inside the Intelligence Services in the 1990s*

Economist, 'Britain's Foreign Office' *Economist* 27 November 1982

Flower, K., *Serving Secretly: An Intelligence Chief On Record—Rhodesia into Zimbabwe 1964-1981* (See relevant British extracts and a good study in its own right of Rhodesian intelligence and foreign policy)*

Foot. M., 'Britain: Intelligence Services' *Economist* 15 March 1980

Gudgin, P., *Military Intelligence: The British Story* (esp. Chapter 3)

Hennessy, P., *Whitehall* (Part Two)*

Hennessy, P., *The Cabinet* ('National Security' chapter)*

Hennessy, P., *The Intellectual Consequences of the Peace**

Herman, M., 'Intelligence and Policy: A Comment' *INS* Vol. 6 No. 1 January, 1991*

Herman, M., *Evaluation of Intelligence: A British Perspective* (Conference Paper)*

Hibbert, R., 'Intelligence and Policy' *INS* January 1990*

Jones, R.V., *Reflections On intelligence*

Lanning, H., Norton-Taylor, R., *A Conflict of Loyalties: GCHO 1984-1991*

Robertson, K.G., (ed) *British and American Approaches To Intelligence**

Rusbridger, J., *The Intelligence Game: Illusions and Delusions of International Espionage*

Seldon, A., 'The Cabinet Office and Coordination 1979-87' *PA* Vol. 68 Spring 1990*

Smith, M. et al., *British Foreign Policy* (Chapter 4 'The Policy-making Process')

Verrier, A., *Through The Looking Glass**

There are a few sources which are tangental to questions relating to policy input and which are of questionable accuracy but aspects of their commentary may be worth consideration:

Bethell, N., *The Great Betrayal*

Bloch, J., Fitzgerald, P., *British Intelligence and Covert Action*

Bower, T., *The Red Web: M16 and the KGB Mastercoup*

Cavendish, A., *Inside Intelligence*

Deacon, R., *A Biography of Sir Maurice Oldfield*

Deacon, R., *British Secret Service*

West, N., *The Friends: Britain's Postwar Secret Intelligence Operations*

West, N., *Games of Intelligence* (Chapter 6)

Also Consult Relevant UK Material on the Reading List for the Falklands Islands and Covert Action Case Studies

Israel

Question *As a very small 'front-line'state Israel's dependence on intelligence for its survival has caused it as many problems as it has brought it benefits. Discuss.*

Beit-Hallani, B., *The Israeli Connection: Who Israel Arms and Why*

Black, I., Morris, B., *Israel's Secret Wars: The Untold Story of Israeli Intelligence**

Blitzer, W., *Between Washington and Jerusalem* (Chapters 1-4, 10-12)

Blitzer, W., *Territory of Lies*

Brecher, M., *The Foreign Policy System of Israel**+(Chapters 6, 7, 10, Part 3)

Brecher, M., *Decisions in Israel's Foreign Policy**+

Cockburn, A. and L., *Dangerous Liaisons: The US-Israeli Covert Relationship*

Cohen, R., 'Threat Assessment in Military Intelligence: The Case of Israel and Syria 1985-1986' *INS* Vol. 4 No. 4 October 1989

Cohen, Y., *Nuclear Ambiguity: The Vanunu Affair*

Cohen. R., 'Israeli Military Intelligence Before the 1956 Sinai Campaign' *INS* January 1988

Deacon, R., *The Israeli Secret Service*+

Doron, G., Pedatzur, R., 'Israeli Intelligence: Utility and Cost Effectiveness' *IJIC* Fall 1989

Doron, G., 'Israeli Intelligence: Tactics, Strategy and Prediction' *IJIC* Fall 1988

Doron, G., Shapira, B., 'Accountability for Secret Operations in

Israel' *IJIC* Fall 1990

Gazit, S., 'Intelligence Estimates and the Decisionmaker' *INS* July 1988*

Hersh, S., *The Samson Option: Israel, America and the Bomb*

Hillel, S., *Operation Babylon Jewish Clandestine Activity in the Middle East 1946-5*

Jacob, A., 'Israel's Military Aid to Africa' *JMAS* Vol. 9 No. 2 1971

Katz, S., *Soldier Spies: Israeli Military Intelligence**

Melman, Y., Raviv, D., *The Imperfect Spies: The History of Israeli intelligence*

Melman, Y., Raviv, D., *Every Spy A Prince : The History of Israeli intelligence**

Ostrovaky, V., Hoy, C., *By Way of Deception: The Making and Unmaking of A Mossad Officer*

Posner, S., *Israel Undercover: Secret Warfare and Hidden Diplomacy in The Middie East*

Steven, S., *The Spymasters of Israel+*

Consult also the Material on Israel from the 'Intelligence Warning and Prediction' Topic

The Canadian and Australian Systems

Question *Why have two small states developed such different intelligence systems? Does this mean that they value the role of intelligence differently?*

Andrew, C., 'The Growth of the Australian Intelligence Community and the Anglo-American Connection' *INS* Vol. 4 No. 2 April 1989*

Ball. D., Richeison, J., *The Ties That Bind: Intelligence Cooperation*

Between The UKUSA Countries (Chapters 3 and 5)*

Canadian Government, *Canadian Security Intelligence Services Act 1989*

CSIS, *The Canadian Security Intelligence Service**

Cieroux, R., *Official Secrets: The Story Behind The Canadian Security Intelligence Service* (Chapters 8, 9, 10)

French, R., Beliveau, A., *The RCMP and the Management of National Security*

Hall, R., *The Secret State**

Mathams, R., *Sub Rosa: Memoirs of An Australian Intelligence Analyst**

Parliamentary Review Committee, *Canadian Security Intelligence Service: Public Report 1991*

Parliamentary Review Committee, *Canadian Security Intelligence Service: Public Report 1992*

Richelson, J., *Foreign Intelligence Organisations* (Chapter 3)

Robertson, K., 'Canadian Intelligence Policy: The Role and Future of CSIS' *IJIC* Vol. 3 No. 2 Summer 1989

Royal Commission of Australias, Security and Intelligence Agencies, *General Report December 1984*

Royal Commission of Australia, *Intelligence and Security* First, Second, Third and Fourth Reports (2 Vols.) 1977

Solicitor General of Canada, *Annual Statement on National Security 1993*

St. John, P., 'Canada's Accession To The Allied Intelligence Community' *CQ* No. 4 1984

Toohey, B., Pinwill, W., *Oyster: The Story of the Australian Secret Intelligence Service*

Whitaker, R., 'Origins of the Canadian Government's Internal Security Programme' *CHR* 1984

Whitaker, R., 'The Politics of Security intelligence Policy-Making in Canada 1970-1984' *INS* Vol. 6 No. 4 October 1991*

Whitaker, R., 'The Politics of Security Intelligence Policy-Making in
Canada: II 1986-91' *INS* Vol. 7 No. 2 April 1992*

Intelligence Warning and Prediction

Question *How do we assess 'failure' when it comes to intelligence
assessment and prediction? Can anything be done to minimise such
occurrences?*

Bar-Joseph, U., 'Methodological Magic' *INS* Vol. 3 No. 4 October
1988*

Ben-Zvi, A., 'Between Warning and Response: The Case of the Yom
Kippur War' *IJIC* Vol. 4 No. 2 Summer 1990

Betts, R., 'Surprise Despite Warning: Why Sudden Attacks Succeed'
PSQ Winter 1980-81

Betts, R., 'Analysis, War and Decision:Why Intelligence Failures
Are Inevitable' *WP* 1978*

Blum, R., 'Surprised by Tito: The Anatomy of An Intelligence
Failure' *Diplomatic History* Vol. 12 Winter 1988

Chan, S., 'The Intelligence of Stupidity: Understanding Failures in
Strategic Warning' *APSR* March 1979*

Cohen, E., 'Only Half A Battle: American Intelligence and Chinese
Intervention in Korea, 1950' *INS* Vol. 5 No. 1 January 1990

Forum, 'Intelligence and Crsis Forecasting' *Orbis* Winter 1983

Handel. M., *War, Strategy and Intelligence* (Chapters 5 and 6)

Handel, M., 'Surprise and Change in International Politics' *IS*
Spring 1980*

Handel, M., 'The Yom Kippur War and the Inevitability of
Surprise' *ISQ* September 1977

Kahn, D., 'The Intelligence Failure of Pearl Harbour' *FA* Vol. 70 No.
5 Winter 1991-92

Kam, E., *Surprise Attack: The Victim's Perspective*

Knorr, K., 'Failures in National Intelligence Estimates: Case of the Cuban Missiles' *WP* April 1964

Levite, A., *Intelligence and Strategic Surprises*

Pfaltzgraf, R., Ra'anan, U., *Intelligence and National Security* (Chapter 7)

Rip, M., Fontanella, J., 'A Window on the Arab-Israeli Yom Kippur War of October 1973: Military Photo-reconnaissance from High Altitude and Space' *INS* Vol. 6 No. 1 January 1991

Shlaim, A., 'Failure in National Intelligence Estimates: The Case of the Yom Kippur War' *WP* April 1976

Stein, J., 'Intelligence and Stupidity Reconsidered: Estimation and Decision in Israel 1973' *JSS* September 1980

Temple, H., *Deaf Captains: Intelligence Policy and the Origins of the Korean War* (Conference Paper)

Wasserman, B., 'The Failure of Intelligence Prediction' *PS* No. 2 1960

Williams, P., 'Intelligence Failures in National Security Policy' *RAF Quarterly* 1974

Wirtz, J., *The Tet Offensive: Intelligence Failure in War*

Wirtz, J., 'Intelligence To Please: The Order of Battle Controversy During the Vietnam War' *PSQ* Vol. 106 No. 2 1991

Wirtz, T., 'The Intelligence Paradigm' *INS* Vol. 4 No. 4 October 1989*

Wohlstetter, R., 'Cuba and Pearl Harbour: Hindsight and Foresight' *FA* July 1965

British Intelligence and the Falkland Islands 1982

Question *'The Falkland islands affair is a prime example of the limitations of intelligence' To what extent is this statement true?*

Cavalinin, E., 'The Malvinas/Falklands Affair: A New Look' *IJIC* Summer 1988

Danchev, A. (ed), *International Perspectives or the Falklands Conflict**

Dillon, G.M., *The Falklands, Politics and War* (Chapters 2, 5 and 6)*

Franks, Lord *Falkland Islands Review* (The Franks Report)

Freedman, L., Gamba-Stonehouse, V., *Signals of War: The Falklands Conflict of 1982**

Freedman, L., 'Intelligence Operations in the Falklands' *INS* September 1986

Herman, M., 'Intelligence Warning of the Occupation of the Falklands: Some Organisational Issues' in Danchev, A., *International Perspectives on the Falklands Conflict*

Hopple, G., 'Intelligence and Warning Lessons: The Falklands' in Watson, Dunn (eds), *Military Lessons of the Falklands War**

Hopple, G., 'Intelligence and Warning: Implications and Lessons of the Falklands Islands War' *WP* April 1984

Hunt, R., *My Falkland Days*

King, D., 'Intelligence Failure and the Falklands War: A Reassessment' *INS* April 1987*

Middlebrook, M., *Taskforce: The Falklands War 1982**

Middlebrook, M., *The Battle for the Malvinas*

Seymour-Ure, C., 'British "War Cabinets" in Limited Wars: Korea, Suez and the Falklands' *Public Administration* Summer 1984*

Sunday Times Insight Team, *The Falklands War*

Wallace, W., 'How Frank Was Franks?' *IA* 1983

White, H., *Lord Franks, The Falklands and the Use of Intelligence* (Seminar Paper)

Williams, P., 'Miscalculation, Crisis management and thd Falklands Conflict' *WT* 1983

US Intelligence and US Policy Towards Iran

Question *The post war US involvement with Iran demonstrates how the proper role and uses of intelligence can be corrupted by other factors. Is this a reasonable view of US intelligence, its performance and US policy regarding Iran?*

Bill, E., *The Eagle and the Lion: America and Iran**

Bradlee, B., *Guts and Glory: The Rise and Fall of Ollver North**

Copeland, M., *The Game Player: Confessions of the CIA's Original Political Operative*

Epstein, E., 'Secrets From the CIA Archive in Tehran' *Orbis* Spring 1987

Gasiorowski, M., 'The 1953 Coup D'Etat in Iran' *IJMES* Vol. 19 1987

Gasiorowski, M., 'Security Relations between the US and Iran 1953-78' in Gasiorowski, Keddie (eds) *Neither East or West*

Irani, R., 'The US involvement in Iran 1942-44' *IRIR* No. 7 1976

Karabell, Z., 'Inside the Espionage Den: The US Embassy and the Fall of the Shah' *INS* Vol. 8 No. 1 1993*

Kornbluh, P., 'The Iran-Contra Scandal: A Postmortem' *WPJ* Winter 1987-88

Ladjevardi, H., 'The Origins of US Support for an Autocratic Iran" *IJMES* Vol. 15 1983

Ledeen, M., Lewis, W., 'Carter and the Fall of the Shah' *WQ* Spring 1980

Moens, A., 'President Carter's Advisers and the Fall of the Shah' *PSQ* Vol. 106 No. 2 1991*

Melbourne, R., 'America and Iran Perspective' *FSJ* 1980

Perry, M., *Eclipse: The Last Days of the CIA* (Part 3)*

Roosevelt, K., *Countercoup: The Struggle For Control of Iran*

Rubin, B., *Paved With Good Intentions: America's Experience in Iran**

Sick, G., *All Fall Down: America's Fateful Encounter With Iran**

Strong, R., 'October Surprises' *INS* Vol. 8 No. 2 April 1993*

Taheri, A., *Nest of Spies: America's Journey To Disaster in Iran**

US House of Representatives, Select Committee on Intelligence, *Iran: Evaluation of US Intelligence Performance Prior To November 1978**

US Intelligence and Estimating the Soviet Strategic Threat

Question *Have post war intelligence estimates of the 'Soviet threat' been 'sucessful' and 'accurate'? Give reasons for your view.*

Becker, A., *CIA Eatimates of Soviet Military Expenditure* Rand P-6534

Burrows, W., *Deep Black: Space Espionage and National Security**

Collins, J., *US Defense Policy: A Critique* (Chapter 11 'Strategic Intelligence')

Forum, 'Soviet Defence Spending' *Problems of Communism* March-April 1985

Freedman, L., *US Intelligence and the Soviet Strategic Threat**

Heuser, B., 'NSC 68 and the Soviet Threat' *IS* Vol. 17 1991*

Hofman, P., 'The Making of National Estimates During the Missile Gap' *INS* September 1986*

Holzman, F., 'Soviet Military Spending: Assessing the Numbers Game' *IS* Spring 1982

Holzman, F., 'Politics and Guesswork: CIA and DIA Estimates of Soviet Military Spending' *IS* Fall 1989*

Jacobsen, C., 'Soviet Defense Costs-The Unquantifiable Burden?' *JPR* No. 4 1987

Jacobsen, C., *The Soviet Defence Enigma*

Kaufman, R., 'Causes of the Slowdown in Soviet Defense' *Survival* No. 4 1985

Laquer, W., The World of Secrets (Chapter 5 'Strategic Estimates')*

Makinen, R., 'The "Sovietisation" of the English Language' *Defence Analysis* No. 1 1985

Pipes, R., 'Team B: The Reality Behind the Myth' *Commentary* October 1986

Prados, J., *The Soviet Estimate: US Intelligence Analysis and Soviet Strategic Forces**

Rosefielde, S., *False Science: Underatanding the Soviet Arms Buildup**

Steiner, B., 'American Intelligence and the Soviet ICBM Build-up: Another Look' *INS* Vol. 8 No. 2 April 1993*

Towle, P., Estimating Foreign Military Power

Twining, D., 'Soviet Strategic Culture: The Missing Dimension' *INS* January 1989

US Congress, Select Committee on Intelligence, *The National Intelligence Estimates A-B Team Episode Concerning Soviet Strategic Capability and Objectives**

US House Armed Services Committee on Intelligence, *Statement By Director of US Naval Intelligence 1989*

Wells, S., 'Sounding the Tocsin: NSC 68 and the Soviet Threat' *IS* Fall 1979*

Covert Action as a Foreign Policy Instrument

Material listed below is in the nature of general reading on covert operations and policy and is also mainly geared to the US experience. Material which covers the UK, Australian and Israeli experience can be found on those respective topic lists.

Question *Is covert action as counter-productive as many of its crit-*

ics contend?

Adler, E., 'Executive Command and Control in Foreign Policy: The CIA's Covert Activities' *Orbis* Fall 1979

Barnes, T., 'The Secret Cold War: The CIA and American Foreign Policy in Europe 1947-1956 Part 1' *HJ* No. 2 1981

Barnes, T., 'The Secret Cold War: The CIA and American Foreign Policy in Europe 1947-1956 part 2' *HJ* No. 3 1982

Barnes, T., 'Democratic Deception: American Covert Operations in Post War Europe' in Carters, D., Tugwell, M., *Deception Operations: Studies In The East-West Context**

Bloomfield, L., 'The Legitimacy of Covert Action: Sorting Out the Moral Responsibilities' *IJIC* Vol. 4 No. 4 Winter 1990

Blum, W., *CIA: The Forgotten History*

Chomeau, J., 'Covert Action's Proper Role in US Policy' *IJIC* Fall 1988

Cockburn, L., *Out of Control: The Reagan Administration's Secret War in Nicaragua*

Colby, W., 'Public Policy: Secret Action' *EIA* Vol. 3 1989

Copeland, M., *The Game Player: Confessions of the CIA's Original Political Operative*

Faligot, R., Krop, P., *La Piscine: The French Secret Services since 1944*

Forsyth, D., 'Democracy, War and Covert Action' *JPR* Vol. 29 No. 4 1992**

Godson, R., (ed) *Intelligence Requirements for the 1980s Vol. 4: Covert Action**

Halperin, M., 'Covert Operations: Effects Of Secrecy On Decisionmaking' in Brosage, Marks (eds) *The CIA File*

Halperin, M., 'Secrecy and Covert Intelligence Collection and Operations' in Halperin, *National Security Policy Making* (Chapter 8)

Lemarchand, R., 'The CIA in Africa' *JMAS* September 1976

Little, D., 'Cold War And Covert Action: The United States And Syria 1945-58' *MEJ* Winter 1990

Lucas, W., 'The Other Collusion: Operation Straggle and Anglo-American Intervention in Syria 1955-56' *INS* July 1989*

Marshall et al, *Iran-Contra Connection: Secret Teams and Covert Operations in the Reagan Era*

Meyer, C., *Facing Reality*+

Miller, J., 'Taking Off The Gloves: The United States And The Italian Elections Of 1948' *DH* Winter 1987

Paterson, T., 'Oversight or Afterview? Congress, The CIA and Covert Actions Since 1947' in Barnhart, M., (ed) *Congress and US Foreign Policy*

Prados, J., *The President's Secret Wars**

Report. *ITT-CIA: Subversion in Chile*+

Rositzke, H., 'America's Secret Operations: A Perspective' *FA* January 1975

Snepp. F., *Decent Interval*

Stockwell, J., *In Search Of Enemies: A CIA Story*+

Sunday Times Insight Team, *The Rainbow Warrior: The French Attempt To Sink Greenpeace*

Treverton, G., *Covert Action: The Limits of Intervention In The Post War World**

US Congress, Select Committee on Intelligence, *Covert Action in Chile 1963-1973*

Weissman, S., 'CIA Covert Action in Zaire and Angola: Patterns and Consequences' *PSQ* Summer 1979

Woodward, B., *Vell: The Secret Wars of CIA 1981-1987*

Democracies and Intelligence Agencies

Question *What are the problems for democracies in having intelli-*

gence communities? And what are the consequences for the relationship between intelligence agencies and democratically elected governments?

Barendt, E., 'Spycatcher and Freedom of Speech' *PL* Summer 1989

Barnds, W., 'Intelligence and Foreign Policy: Dilemmas of A Democracy' *FA* January 1969*

Blais, J., 'The Political Accountability of Intelligence Agencies-Canada' *INS* January 1989*

Bruce Lockhart, J., 'The Relationship Between Secret Services and Government in A Modern State' *RUSI* March 1974

Bruce Lockhart, J., 'Secret Services and Democracy' *Brassey's Defence Annual 1974*

Cohen, W., 'Congressional Oversight of Covert Action' *IJIC* Summer 1988

Cripps, Y., 'Disclosure and the Public Interest' *PL* Summer 1985

Emerson, T., 'Control of Government Intelligence Agencies—The American Experience' *TPQ* Vol. 53 1982

Feldman, D., 'Constitutional Dimensions of the Iran-Contra Affair' *IJIC* Fall 1988

Franck, T., Eisen, J., 'Balancing National Security and Free Speech' *JILP* Winter 1982

Gill, P., 'Symbolic or Peal? The Impact of the Canadian Security Intelligence Review Committee 1984-88' *INS* July 1989

Godfrey, E., 'Ethics and Intelligence' *FA* April 1978*

Griffith, J., 'The Official Secrets Act' *JLS* Autumn 1989

Hastedt, G., 'The Constitutional Control of Intelligence' *INS* May 1986*

Hastedt, G., *Controlling Intelligence**

Jackson, W., 'Congressional Oversight of Intelligence: Search for A Framework' *INS* July 1990

Johnson, L., *A Season Of Inquiry: The Congressional Intelligence Investigation*

Johnson, L., 'Covert Action and Accountability: Decisionmaking for America's Secret Foreign Policy' *ISQ* Vol. 33 1989

Johnson, L., 'Controlling the CIA: A Critique of Current Safeguards' *HJLPP* Vol. 12 1989

Johnson, L., 'Legislative Reform of Intelligence Policy' *Polity* Spring 1985

Johnson, L., 'The US Congress and the CIA: Monitoring the Dark Side of Government' *LSQ* Vol. 5 1980

Jordan, K., 'Extent of the Independent Presidential Authority to Conduct Foreign Intelligence Activities' *GLJ* Vol. 72 1984

Karalekas, A., 'Intelligence Oversight: Has Anything Changed?' *WQ* Summer 1983

Liberal Party Intelligence Services Working Group, *Liberty and Security*

Maechling, G., 'Official Secrets: British Style/American Style' *IJIC* Fall 1988*

Mates, M., *The Secret Services. Is There A Case For Greater Openness?*

Rankin, M., 'National Security: Information, Accountability and the Canadian Security Intelligence Service' *UTLJ* 1986

Robertson, K., 'Accountable Intelligence-The British Experience' *CQ* Winter 1988

Robertson, K., *Intelligence. Terrorism and Civil Liberties* (Paper)

Robertson, K., (ed) *British and American Approaches To Intelligence* (Chapters 9, 10 and 11)*

Scolville, H., 'Is Espionage Necessary For Our Security?' *FA* April 1976*

Thomas, R., *Espionage and Secrecy*

Treverton, G., 'Imposing A Standard: Covert Action and American Democracy' *EIA* Vol. 3 1989

Turner, S., *Secrecy and Democracy*

Turner, S., Thibault, G., 'Intelligence: The Right Rules' *FP* 1983

Weller, G., 'Accountability in the Canadian Intelligence Services'

IJIC Fall 1988*

Intelligence and Terrorism

Question *'The best defence against terrorismis good intelligence.'*
Discuss.

Andersen, M., *Policing the World: Interpol and the Politics of International Police Cooperation* (Chapter 6 'The Terrorist Factor')*

Beitler, S., 'Counterintelligence and Combatting Terrorism' in Hopple and Watson, *The Military Intelligence Community**

Bresler, F., *Interpol*

Celmer, M., 'The Intelligence Community and Terrorism' in Celmer, *Terrorism, US Strategy and Reagan's Policies*

Charters, D., 'Intelligence and Psychological Warfare Operations in Northern Ireland' *RUSI* 1977

Cooper, H., 'Terrorism and the Intelligence Function' in Livingston, M(ed) *International Terrorism in the Contemporary World*

Cowan, W., 'Intelligence Rescue, Retaliation and Decision Making' in Rubin, B., *Terrorism and Politics*

Crabtree, R., 'US Policy on Counterterrorism: The Intelligence Dimension' *CQ* Winter 1986

Davidson Smith, G., *Combating Terrorism* (Chapter 3 'Decision Making and Crisis Management Machinery')*

Davidson Smith, G., 'Canada's Counter-Terrorism Experience' *TPV* Vol. 5 No. 1 Spring 1993*

Forum, 'Intelligence and Counterterrorism' *Orbis* Vol. 28 No. 1 Spring 1984*

Gazit, S., Handel, M., 'Insurgency, Terrorism and *Intelligence'* in Godson, R., (ed) *Intelligence Requirements for the 1980s:*

Counterintelligence*

Jeffrey, K., 'Intelligence and Counter-Insurgency Operations: Some Reflections On The British Experience' *INS* Vol. 2 No. 1 January 1987

Jenkins, P., 'The Assassins Revisited : Claire Sterling and the Politics of Intelligence' *INS* 1989

Heather, R., 'Intelligence and Counter-Insurgency in Kenya, 1952-56' *INS* July 1990

House of Commons, Home Affairs Committee, 7th Report, *Practical Police Cooperation in the European Communities Vol. 1**

Kerstetter, W., 'Terrorism and Intelligence' *Terrorism* Vol. 3 1979

Kitson, F., *Low Intensity Operations* (Chapter 6 'Tactics: The Handling of Information')

Maguire, K., 'The Intelligence War in Northern Ireland' *IJIC* Vol. 4 No. 2 Summer 1990

Motley, J., 'International Terrorism: A Challenge for US Intelligence' *IJIC* Spring 1986

Murphy, J., 'Intelligence and State Support of International Terrorism' in Murphy, J., *State Support of International Terrorism*

Oseth, J., 'Intelligence and Low Intensity Conflict' *USNWCR* No. 37 1984

Robertson, K., *Intelligence, Terrorism and Civil Liberties* (Conference paper)

Schoelwer, M., 'The Future of the US Intelligence Community in Low Intensity Conflict' in Thompson, L., *Low Intensity Conflict*

Sloan, S., 'US Anti-Terrorism Policies: Lessons To Be Learned To Meet An Enduring and Changing Threat' *TPV* Vol. 5 No. 1 Spring 1993*

Sulc, L., 'Terrorism and the Importance of Intelligence' *Terrorism* Vol. 10 1987

Taylor, R., 'Terrorism and Intelligence' *Defense Analysis* Vol. 3 No. 2 1987

TVI Staff, 'Interpol's Response to *Terrorism*' Terrorism Summer 1985

Urban, M., *Big Boys' Rules: The Secret Struggle Against the IRA*

Various authors, 'Terrorism and the Intelligence Policy Process' in Cimbala, S., (ed) *Intelligence and Intelligence Policy In a Democratic Society**

Wardlaw, G., 'The Place of Intelligence' in Wardlaw, G., *Political Terrorism**

Whitaker, R., 'Apprehended Intelligence: The RCMP and the October Crisis' *Queen's Quarterly* Summer 1993*

Wolf, J., 'Antiterrorist Intelligence' in Wolf, J., *Antiterrorist Initiatives*

Western Intelligence, Iraq and the Gulf War

Question *Applying what you now know concerning intelligence and policy give reasons for Western governments' apparent surprise at Iraq's invasion of Kuwait and evaluate the performance of 'Western Intelligence' on Iraq before, during and after the Gulf War*

Charters, D., *Operational and Tactical Intelligence in DESERT STORM: A Case Study of Inter-Agency Cooperation* (Conference Paper)

Cowley, C., *Guns, Lies and Spies*

Darwish, A., Alexander, G., *Unholy Babylon: The Secret History of Saddam's War**

De La Billiere, P., *Storm Command: A Personal Account of the Gulf War*

George, A., 'The Persian Gulf Crisis, 1990-91' in A. George (ed) *Avoiding War: The Role of Crisis Management*

Leadbetter, W., Bury, S., 'Prelude To Desert Storm: The

Politicisation of Intelligence' *IJIC* Vol. 6 No. 1 Spring 1993*
Leigh, D., *Betrayed: The Matrix Churchill Story**
Sweeney, J., *Trading With The Enemy: Britain's Arming of Iraq*
Taylor, S., Ralston, T., 'The Role of Intelligence in Crisis Management' in A. George (ed) *Avoiding War: The Role of Crisis Management**
Timmerman, K., *The Death Lobby: How the West Armed Iraq**
Watson, B., George, B., et al., *Military Lessons of the Gulf War*
Woodward, B., *The Commanders**

Intelligence and the Post Cold War World

Question *What are the uses of, and issues for, "intelligence" in the Post Cold War World?*

Andreas, P., 'Dead End Drug Wars' *FP* No. 85 1991-92
Berkowitz, B., Goodman, A., 'Why Spy and How in the 1990s?' *Orbis* Vol. 36 No. 2 Spring 1992*
Boren, D., 'The intelligence Community: How Crucial?' *FA* Vol. 71 No. 3 Summer 1992
Carver, G., 'Intelligence and Glasnost' *FA* Summer 1990*
Clapper, J., Lt. Col., 'Defense Intelligence Reorganisation and Challenges' *DIJ* Vol. 1 No. 1 1992
Codevilla, A., *Informing Statecraft: Intelligence for a New Century**
Colby, W., 'Tactical Intelligence: The Need For Improvement' *DIJ* Vol. 1 No. 1 1992
Dabelko, G., *The US Intelligence Community and the International Environment* (Conference Paper)
Dabelko, D., Dabelko. G., 'The International Environment and the US Intelligence Community' *IJIC* Vol. 6 No. 1 Spring 1993*
De Marenches, A., *The Fourth World War: Diplomacy and Espionage*

in the Age of Terrorism (Chapters 7-12)*

Farson, Stafford, Wark, *Security and Intelligence and Changing World-New Perspectives for the 1990s**

Gates, R., 'Address to Nixon Library Conference' *USIS* 1992

Herman, M., 'Governmental Intelligence: Its Evolution and Role' *JESI* Vol. 2 No. 2 1992

Huinick, A., *Intelligence Cooperation in the Post Cold War Era: Will There Be A New Game Plan?* (Conference paper)

Johnson, L., 'Smart Intelligence' *FP* No. 89 Winter 1992-93*

Krepon, M., 'Glasnost and Multilateral Verification: Implications for the US Intelligence Community' *IJIC* Vol. 4 No. 1 Spring 1990

Mathews, J., 'Redefining Security' *FA* Vol. 68 Spring 1989*

Macartney, J., *Peacekeeping and Intelligence* (Conference Paper)

May, E., 'Intelligence: Backing into the Future' *FA* Vol. 71 No. 3 Summer 1992*

Scalingi, P., 'Managing Intelligence in an Age of Uncertainty: Refocusing To Meet the Challenge' *WQ* Winter 1992

Schweizer, P., *Friendly Spies: The Uses of Economic Espionage*

Shulsky, A., *What is Intelligence?**

Turner, S., 'Intelligence for a New World Order' *FA* Vol. 70 Fall 1991*

Uliman, R., 'Redefining Security' *IS* Vol. 8 Summer 1983

Wark, W. et al., 'The Future of Espionage' *Queen's Quarterly* Summer 1993*

Watson, P., *The FBI's Changing Missions in the 1990s* (CSI Working Paper)

Wirtz, J., 'Miscalculation, Surprise and American Intelligence After the Cold War' *IJIC* Vol. 5 No. 1 Spring 1991

Wright, J., 'Intelligence and Economic Security' *IJIC* Vol. 5 No. 2 Summer 1991*

Post-Cold War, Democratization, and National Intelligence:
Comparative Perspectives

October 13-14, 1995
Seoraksan-room, Hilton Hotel, Seoul

Hosted by
The Korean Society for the Study of National Intelligence(KSSNI)

Sponsored by
Kisan, Daewoo Heavy Industries Ltd., Korean Airlines,
Seoul Broadcasting System, Sisa Journal, The Joong Ang Daily News

General Information

1. Participants from home and abroad should register at the desk in front of the Seoraksan-room at 9:00 A.M., Friday, October 13.
2. During the Conference, you can obtain help from the secretariat.
3. Papers will be sold at the desk on conference day.
4. For productive and effective sessions, the allocated time for paper presentations and discussion is as follows:
Paper presentation: 20-25 min.
Discussion   : 8-10 min.

Registration and Opening Ceremony

October 13 (Fri)

09:00-09:30   **Registration**

09:30-09:30   **Opening Ceremony**
- Opening Remarks: Jin-hyun Kim, President of the KSSNI
- Congratulatory Remarks:
  - **William E. Colby**(former director of CIA)
  - **Vadim A. Kirpitchenko**(Chairman of Advisory Board, Russian Foreign Intelligence Service)

Panel Meetings

10:00-12:30

Panel 1: "Democratization and National Intelligence:
Theory and Practice"
Chair: Dalchoong Kim, Yonsei University
Panelists:
  (1) "Democratic System and National Intelligence: American Experience in Comparative Perspectives"
  William E. Colby, Former Director of CIA
  (2) "Perestroika, Glasnost, and KGB: Surviving Democratic Currents"
  General **Vadim A. Kirpitchenko,** Chairman of Advisory Board, Russian Foreign Intelligence Service
Discussants:
  (1) **Tong Whan Park,** Northwestern University
  (2) **Jeong-woo Kihl,** The Joong Ang Daily News

12:30-14:00 Lunch hosted by Young Suk Yoon, Chairman and CEO of DAEWOO Heavy Industries, Ltd.

14:00-17:30

Panel 2: "Changing World Order and Reforming National Intelligence: Comparative Perspectives"
Chair: Jung-suk Youn, Chung Ang University
Panelists:
  (1) "Changing U.S. International Interests and Priorities: Implications for Intelligence Reforms"
  W. Bruce Weinrod, Former Deputy Assistant Secretary of

Defense for International Security Policy

(2) "An Israeli Perspective on Contemporary National Intelligence"

General **Aviezer Yaari,** Head of Defense Auditing, Israeli Comptroller's Office

(3) "Redefining National Priority and Intelligence in South Korea"

Chung-in Moon, Yonsei University

In-Taek Hyun, Korea University

Woosang Kim, Sookmyung Women's University

Jung-hoon Lee, Yonsei University

Discussants:

(1) **Gahp Chol Kim,** Konkuk University

(2) **Jong-chun Baek,** The Sejong Institute

October 14 (Sat)

09:30-12:30

Panel 3: "Rethinking National Intelligence and the Private Sector: Myth and Reality on Non-Military Espionage"

Chair: Young-Sun Ha, Seoul National University

Panelists:

(1) "Economic Espionage and Counter-Espionage in the United States: The Threat and The Policy Response"

William T. Warner, CSIS

(2) "Trade Secrets, UR Efforts, and Korea's Position"

Jang-Hee Yoo, President of Korea Institute for International Economic Policy

(3) "Economic Intelligence in Japan"

Akio Kasai, Advisor to Itochu and Former Senior Member of Japan's Cabinet Intelligence Office

Discussants:

(1) **In-Joung Whang,** Former Director of Korea Development Institute

(2) **Chung-min Lee,** Rand Corporation

12:30-14:00 **Lunch hosted by Shin-Heung Lee, President of Kisan.**

14:00-16:00

Panel 4: **"Roundtable on Restructuring National Intelligence in South Korea"**

Moderator: **Chung-in Moon,** Yonsei University

Participants: all panelists

Korean Society for the Study of National Intelligence

\# 320 Yonhee Hall, Office of Professor Chung-in Moon

Department of Political Science, Yonsei University

134 Shinchon-dong, Sodaemoon-ku, Seoul 120-749, Korea

Tel: (82-2) 361-2953   Fax: (82-2) 365-5524

Index

[About Editors]

Jin-hyun Kim is President of the Seoul City University and President of the Korean Society for the Study of National Intelligence. He was Minister of Science and Technology of the Republic of Korea.

Chung-in Moon is Professor of Political Science at Yonsei University and Executive Secretary of the Korean Society for the Study of National Intelligence.

[About Contributors]

William E. Colby was Director of Central Intelligence Agency (CIA) from 1973 to 1976. He is currently Counsel to the law firm of Donovan Leisure Newton & Irvin as well as Editor of the Colby Report for International Business.

Vadim A. Kirpitchenko is Chairman of the Advisory Board of the Russian Foreign Intelligence. He served as First Vice Chairman of the First Directorate of the KGB in the former Soviet Union.

W. Bruce Weinrod is a Washington, D.C.-based attorney and an Adjunct Fellow at the Center for Strategic and International Studies. He served as Deputy Assistant Secretary of Defense for European and NATO affairs.

Aviezer Yaari is Head of Defense and Security Department, State Comptroller's Office of Israel. He served as Commandant of the Israeli National Defense College and Deputy Director of Military Intelligence, the Israeli Defense Forces.

In-Taek Hyun is Assistant Professor of Political Science at Korea University. He was Senior Fellow of the Sejong Institute.

Woosang Kim is Associate Professor of Political Science at Sookmyung Women's University. He previously taught at Texas A&M University.

Jung-hoon Lee is Assistant Professor of International Relations at the Graduate School of International Relations, Yonsei University. He held teaching and research positions at the University of California at Berkeley and University of Tokyo.

Akio Kasai is an advisor to Itochu Corporation. He served as a senior official at the Japanese Cabinet Intelligence and Research Office.

William T. Warner is an attorney and a former US naval intelligence officer. He has written extensively on economic and technology espionage.

Jang-Hee Yoo is President of Korea Institute for International Economic Policy. He is a member of the Foreign Policy Advisory Committee, Segyehwa Promotion Committee, and the Korea-America 21st Century Council.

Judy E. Chung is a graduate student at the Graduate School of International Relations, Yonsei University. She holds her B.A. from Columbia University and has worked as a student journalist.